Witches,
WENCHES &
WILD WOMEN
OF RHODE ISLAND

Witches, WENCHES & WILD WOMEN
OF RHODE ISLAND

M.E. REILLY-MCGREEN

THE
History
PRESS

Published by The History Press
Charleston, SC 29403
www.historypress.net

Copyright © 2010 by M.E. Reilly-McGreen
All rights reserved

First published 2010
Second printing 2010
Third printing 2011
Fourth printing 2012

ISBN 9781540224149

Library of Congress Cataloging-in-Publication Data

Reilly-McGreen, M. E.
Witches, wenches, and wild women of Rhode Island / M.E. Reilly-McGreen.
p. cm.
Includes bibliographical references.

1. Women--Rhode Island--Biography. 2. Witches--Rhode Island--Biography. 3. Rhode
Island--Biography. I. Title.
CT3262.R4R45 2010
920.7209745--dc22
2010013683

To Joe, Reilly, Colin and Peter

CONTENTS

CONTENTS

ACKNOWLEDGEMENTS

First, to my boys—Reilly, Colin and Peter McGreen—thank you for your love, your encouragement, your patience and your understanding. Also, thank you to Peter and Joyce Reilly, my parents, who have always had more faith in me than I had in myself. To my siblings and best friends—Sean Reilly, Tim Reilly, Kate Grosso and Tara Sanda—thank you for your staunch support and restraint from making comments about similarities between me and my subject matter. Thank you, too, to Donna Shirley Reilly, my sister in spirit, for her endless enthusiasm about anything involving ghosts, vampires or witches. And to my dear sisters-in-law, Katherine and Anna McGreen, thank you for your unwavering encouragement.

A number of friends also assisted in gathering information and providing photographs. James and Tracey Manni, thank you so much for the beautiful Block Island photographs, as well as all your knowledge of the island, its inhabitants, its legends and its lore. Everyone visiting Block Island should be in the company of such fabulous tour guides. Michael Bell, thank you for letting me tag along. Thank you, too, to Betty Cotter, Carrie DiPrete, Gale Eaton, Susan Graham, Laura Kelly, Mag Ryan and Ericka Tavares for your offers of assistance, your wit and your wisdom.

I also owe a debt of gratitude to the following organizations: the South County Museum, the Newport Historical Society, the Pettaquamscutt Historical Society and the Providence Athenaeum. To the ladies of the Peace Dale Library, Rebecca Turnbaugh and Jessica Wilson, I am deeply grateful and honored that you allowed me access to your special collections and your knowledge. And to Keith Lewis, thank you for sharing your Block Island stories with me.

This book would never have materialized if not for the Chariho School Committee's approval of my course, "Rhode Island Myth, Legend and Folklore." Thank you, as well, to Chariho Regional School District superintendent Barry Ricci, Chariho Regional High School principal Robert Mitchell, Chariho Regional High School assistant principal Elizabeth Sinwell, former Chariho Regional High School assistant principal Philip Auger, PhD, and Chariho Regional High School English Department chair Shelley Kenny for allowing me this privilege. Special thanks, too, to the students of Chariho Regional High School, without whose interest and enthusiasm this course would never have happened.

To all the authors whose work I reviewed in researching and writing this book, thank you.

This book would have been so much poorer without the artistic eye and photographic talents of Mark Kiely. Thank you, Mark, for your vision.

I would like to thank Jeffrey Saraceno, Saunders Robinson and everyone at The History Press for all of your advice and assistance. It has been a wonderful experience working with you.

And to Joe, the most supportive husband a woman could have, thank you for everything.

INTRODUCTION

This is a book about magic, specifically the magic of Rhode Island. I think the best description I've read of Rhode Island's magic is by author John Updike in his bestselling novel *The Witches of Eastwick*:

> *Rhode Island, though famously the smallest of the fifty states, yet contains odd American vastnesses, tracts scarcely explored amid industrial sprawl, abandoned homesteads and forsaken mansions, vacant hinterlands hastily traversed by straight black roads, heathlike marshes and desolate shores on either side of the Bay, that great wedge of water driven like a stake clean to the state's heart, its trustfully named capital. "The fag end of creation" and "the sewer of New England," Cotton Mather called the region. Never meant to be a separate polity, settled by outcasts like the bewitching, soon-to-die Anne Hutchinson, this land holds manifold warps and wrinkles. Its favorite road sign is a pair of arrows pointing either way. Swampy poor in spots, elsewhere it became a playground of the exceedingly rich. Refuge of Quakers and antinomians, those final distillates of Puritanism, it is run by Catholics, whose ruddy Victorian churches loom like freighters in the sea of bastard architecture. There is a kind of metallic green stain, bitten deep into Depression-era shingles, that exists nowhere else. Once you cross the state line, whether at Pawtucket or Westerly, a subtle change occurs, a cheerful dishevelment, a contempt for appearances, a chimerical uncaring. Beyond the clapboard slums yawn lunar stretches where only an abandoned*

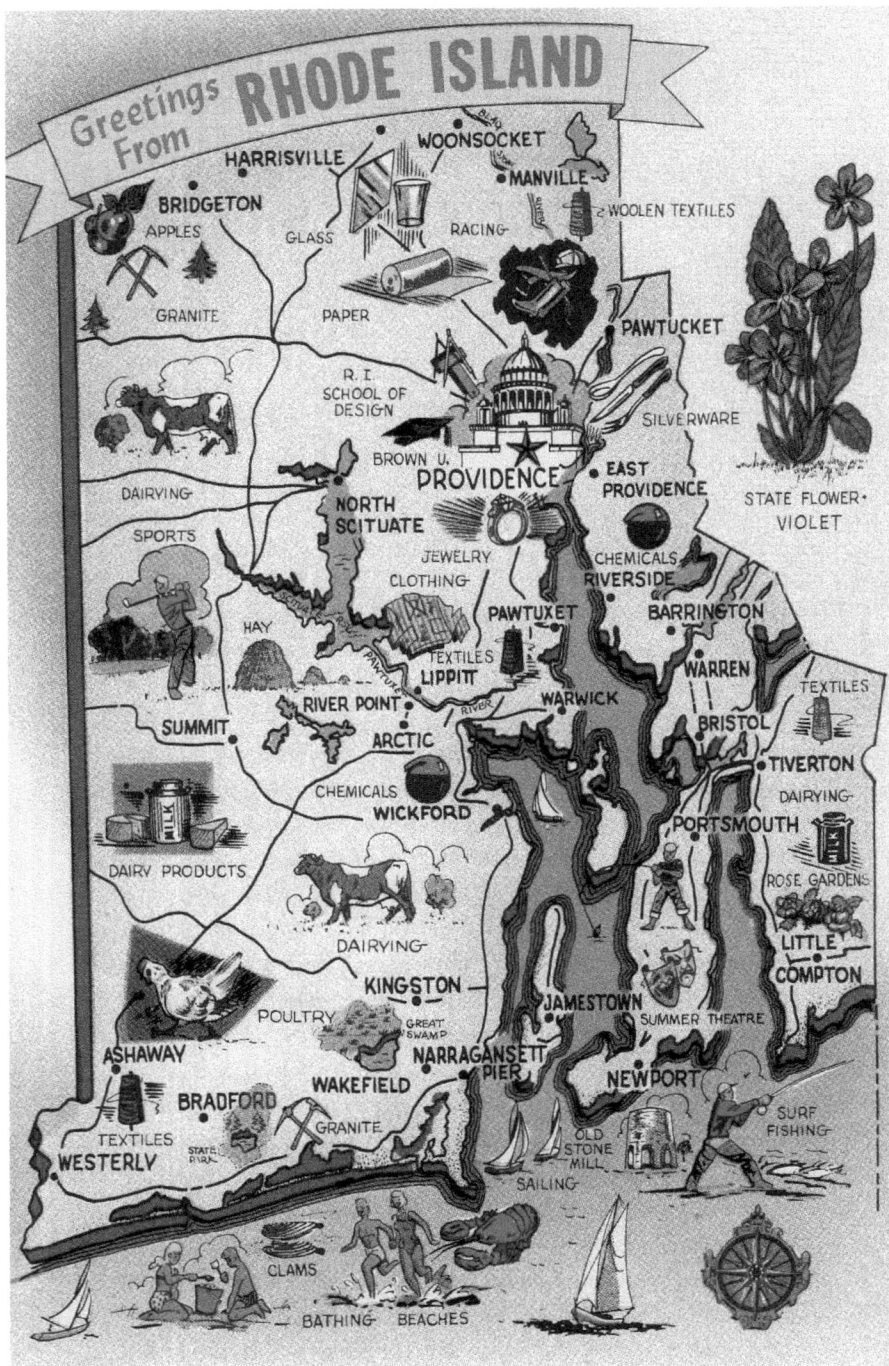

Greetings from Rhode Island. *Author's collection.*

roadside stand offering the ghost of last summer's CUKES betrays the yearning, disruptive presence of man.

Updike chose Rhode Island, specifically Eastwick, a fictional town believed to be composed of equal parts East Greenwich and Wickford, as home for his beloved coven comprising Alexandra Spoffard, Jane Smart, Sukie Rougemont and the devil, Darryl Van Horne. Let Arthur Miller have his Salem and its prepubescent shrews; real witches work their magic in Rhode Island, aka "Rogue's Island."

As a rabid fan of revenants, ghosts and ghouls, I consider myself blessed to have grown up just outside of Wickford and a mile from Exeter, the final resting place of Mercy Brown, America's last vampire. In my twenty-odd years as a journalist, I have taken every opportunity offered to write about the state's strange stories, and there are many. I found witches particularly attractive, as to me, they were women who flouted societal norms and lived by their own rules. Through the years, I have also been privileged to profile many of the state's most accomplished women. From this experience, I learned that the ordinary woman who dared to challenge convention oftentimes found herself labeled a witch as a result.

I didn't begin collecting local stories in earnest until I had the opportunity to teach a class called "Rhode Island Myth, Legend and Folklore" at Chariho Regional High School. I have learned that there are unique job hazards encountered when teaching a class with such a title to teenagers. First, your audience is certain that you, yourself, are a witch. Second, students want to know the answers to questions for which you have no answer, like, "Do you believe in (insert any number of supernatural creatures' names here)?"

What I do believe in is the magic of stories. When as a child I read *The Lion, the Witch and the Wardrobe*, I imagined that a closet could be a portal to another world. I wanted desperately to fly from my bedroom window hand in hand with Peter Pan or to tumble headlong down the rabbit hole with Alice. I admit, even in adulthood, I look to trees to see if Boo Radley might have left me a treasure in a knothole. These characters were my childhood friends and their stories my sustenance. They offered adventure, excitement and always magic.

As an adult, I stand with John Updike in his assessment of Rhode Island. It is a magical place of "chimerical uncaring," loved fiercely by its residents for its contrary nature. Updike wrote, "This air of Eastwick empowered women." I would argue only that he expand his assessment to include the rest of the state. Rhode Island literature and lore offers a treasure-trove of stories of magic, mischief and mayhem equal to anything produced elsewhere. For this book, I focus on stories of Rhode Island's remarkable women, both historical and fictional. Some of the women profiled here are native Rhode Islanders, and some are Gilded Age socialites, Newport's summer elite. One woman may have had only a one-night stand with the Ocean State, but her legend lives on here. Still other women, like Updike's witches, may be entirely fictitious, created solely to serve the interests of a good story. But this is, after all, Rogue's Island. We take all kinds.

On the subject of sibyls and sorceresses, I found we had witches with stories to rival those of Salem. We had wenches whose nefarious natures resulted in stories of mayhem and matricide. And we had wild women, a term I use with the greatest admiration to describe those women who distinguished themselves in their determination to challenge contemporary notions of a woman's place in society. My wild women lobbied for women's rights, fought for peace, braved nature's worst and weathered men's wrath in living according to their consciences.

So when my students ask what I believe, I say I believe in the power of stories to transport, to inspire and even to transform us. I believe in stories of women like Anne Hutchinson and Mary Dyer, who would not allow their voices to be silenced by Puritan persecutors, and Kate Chase Sprague, whose political views were sought by presidents. I think of Ida Lewis, who would strike out across the roughest seas to save those needing saving, and Alva Erskine Vanderbilt Belmont, who traded the socialite's life for that of suffragette. I even believe in *The Witches of Eastwick* for what they represent: a woman's right to live on her terms. And so, when asked what I believe, I smile like Alice's Cheshire Cat and quote Roald Dahl, who said, "Those who don't believe in magic will never find it."

I would add that those inclined to search for it need look no further than their own backyard.

PART I

THIRTEEN WITCHES AND A VAMPIRE

-❄❆❄-

TUGGIE BANNOCK:
NARRAGANSETT'S WOULD-BE WITCH

Perhaps the most menacing figure in witch folklore is the terrible Baba Yaga of Russia. This ancient crone was mercurial in nature. Sometimes she assisted the intrepid youth or maid who crossed her path. Other times she ate those who crossed her. Baba Yaga's other mark of distinction was her home. Built atop giant chicken legs, the old hag's hut was the first mobile home. Don't be fooled by this seemingly comical mode of travel, though. To be menaced by Baba Yaga and her magical conveyance was to tangle with a fearsome and formidable monster.

Baba Yaga was everything Tuggie Bannock wished to be but wasn't.

In all likelihood, Narragansett witch Tuggie Bannock is like Baba Yaga in one respect: she is probably fictional. The resemblance ends there, however. Bannock is a comical figure in local folklore. A former slave, Bannock eked out a living by hiring herself out for odd jobs and telling the occasional fortune. Her troubles came as the result of botched spells and ineffective hexes.

One Bannock story has the old witch angry with a local tinker by the name of Bosum Sidet. Poor old Bosum broke her favorite copper teakettle, and Bannock's wrath was fierce. Alice Morse Earle writes in her book, *In Old Narragansett*, that Bannock's "charm was, alas, a malignant one, a 'conjure' that she angrily decided to work upon him as a revenge." Lest there be any confusion about Bannock's intent, Earle continues, "This charm was not a matter of a moment's hasty decision and careless action; it required some minute and varied preparation and considerable skill to carry it out successfully, and work due and desired evil."

Earle writes that Bannock gathered the charm's necessary ingredients: twigs from a bush by Bosum's house, hairs clipped from the tail of his cow and

> *a few rusty nails, the tail of a smoked herring, a scrap of red flannel, a little mass of "grave dirt" that she had taken from one of the many graveyards that are dotted all over Narragansett, and, last of all, that chief ingredient in all charms—a rabbit's foot...* [These] *were thrown into a pot of water that was hung upon the crane over a roaring fire.*

Bannock's noxious brew suited her appearance on this occasion. Earle describes her as

> *tall and gaunt, with long bony arms, and skinny claws of hands, with a wrinkled, malicious, yet half-frightened countenance, surrounded by little pigtails of gray wool that stuck out from under her scarlet turban...she stood like a Voodoo priestess eagerly watching and listening.*

Still, Bannock was unprepared when an unseen assailant pushed her from behind. She thought she'd conjured a moonack, an evil creature that, legend holds, would strike Bannock dead if she were to look at it. In her moment of terror, the would-be witch turned to prayer, promising to mend her wicked ways if she were spared.

Bannock never saw the four little boys who snuck into her hovel to retrieve the bobsled that had forced her to the floor. She only heard with relief the retreat of some heavy thing as it dragged itself back out her door. When the old witch was sure she was alone, she "tremblingly arose, closed the door, swung the pot off the fire, seized a horseshoe and prayerbook, and went to bed."

It was to old Tinker Bosum's advantage that Tuggie Bannock's charms had a tendency to backfire. No reports of his having come to any harm exist.

◈

Mercy Brown:
Eternally Bewitched and Bedeviled

Mercy Lena Brown a witch? At first blush, it may seem erroneous or, at the very least, odd that Rhode Island's most famous vampire would be called a witch, but folklore doesn't really differentiate between the two. Many cultures believed that witches fed on human blood. The Greek lamia feasted on children. The Russian Baba Yaga also had a bloodlust for children, though she preferred hers roasted. Egyptians, Celts and Europeans had their hags, who would sit on their sleeping victims, feasting on their blood or breath, depending on their preference, in a process called, alternately, hagging or witch riding.

If a witch is defined by her habits, then "witch" is no misnomer when applied to Mercy Brown. She was believed to have fed on her brother, Edwin,

The headstone of Mercy Brown is often bedecked with trinkets and coins from admirers. *Photo by M.E. Reilly-McGreen.*

17

who suffered from a wasting illness called consumption. Consumption had claimed the lives of Edwin's mother, Mary Eliza, his sister, Mary Olive, and, of course, Mercy. The Browns' second daughter died in January 1892. Many members of the rural community of Exeter subscribed to the folk belief that a demon, a revenant, was responsible for the nighttime assaults on Edwin. Moreover, the folk belief held that the demon would reside in the body of a family member (in this case, Mercy).

And so it was folk beliefs that spurred the disinterment and defilement of Mercy's remains in March 1892. Among those present were Mercy's father, George Brown, and the town's medical examiner, Harold Metcalf. The two men did not believe in the folk remedy themselves, and their involvement was likely motivated by pressure from frightened neighbors. George Brown's ordeal with consumption was a decade long at the time of the disinterment of the female members of his family.

According to a March 21, 1892 *Providence Journal* article reprinted in Michael Bell's seminal work *Food for the Dead: On the Trail of New England's Vampires*, Mary Eliza was the first to be disinterred:

> *On Wednesday morning* [March 17], *therefore, the doctor went as desired to what is known as Shrub Hill Cemetery, in Exeter, and found four men who had unearthed the remains of Mrs. Brown, who had been interred four years* [she had been dead for nine years]. *Some of the muscles and flesh still existed in a mummified state, but there were no signs of blood in the heart. The body of the first daughter,* [Mary] *Olive, was then taken out of the grave, but only a skeleton, with a thick growth of hair, remained.*
>
> *Finally the body of* [Mercy] *Lena, the second daughter, was removed from the tomb, where it had been placed till spring. The body was in a fairly well preserved state. It had been buried two months. The heart and liver were removed, and in cutting open the heart, clotted and decomposed blood was found, which was what might be expected at that stage of decomposition. The liver showed no blood, though it was in a well-preserved state. These two organs were removed, and a fire being kindled in the cemetery, they were reduced to ashes, and the attendants seemed satisfied.*

Those present no doubt felt justified in their unholy task when, upon tearing into the nineteen-year-old's chest, heart and liver, they found blood. Poor Mercy's heart was burned on a rock in the Chestnut Hill Cemetery, and, legend says, its ashes were mixed with water and fed to her brother Edwin.

He died anyway. It was Mercy who lived.

A TIMELESS LEGEND

The *Providence Journal*'s headlines about the Brown family's tragedy attracted the attention of the world. A sample:

> EXHUMED THE BODIES.
> *Testing a Horrible Superstition in the Town of Exeter.*
> BODIES OF DEAD RELATIVES TAKEN FROM THEIR GRAVES.
> *They Had All Died of Consumption, and the Belief Was that Live Flesh and Blood Would Be Found that Fed Upon the Bodies of the Living.*

A newspaper clipping about Mercy Lena Brown was found in *Dracula* author Bram Stoker's papers. The author, who lived in Europe, published his novel about the iconic vampire in 1897, five years after the Exeter incident. Stoker scholars maintain that the Irish author learned of Mercy's story after having finished his novel. But that hasn't stopped Mercy's fans from speculating how it is, then, that Lucy and Mina, the two female characters in the novel, bear names strikingly similar to Mercy Lena.

Mercy Brown's story casts a spell whose power endures. In 1979, the *Providence Journal* chronicled a couple's efforts to record Mercy Brown's voice from the grave.

They were unsuccessful. Imagine that.

Their failure doesn't stop others from trying to have their own experience of Mercy. Police routinely patrol the Chestnut Hill Cemetery on Halloween, when Mercy mania reaches its height. Most people are respectful. Offerings are routinely left on her grave—little things like miniature pumpkins, smooth rocks, flowers, glow sticks and silver coins. Mercy's headstone has fallen prey to vandals on occasion and even disappeared for a time. It is now tethered to its marble base by an iron collar anchored to a cement cone. The irony here is that iron is a material abhorred by witches and fairies alike. It burns them much in the same way silver does vampires. Witch or vampire, Mercy would no doubt find neither metal to her liking.

Mercy's influence extends well beyond Exeter even today. In 2008, the History Channel's *Monster Quest* series featured Mercy in an episode entitled "Vampires in America." In 2009, brothers and filmmakers Donald and Paul Mantia of North Providence debuted their forty-minute film *The Last American Vampire: Mercy's Revenge*, made with a budget of $1,200.

In the movie, Mercy rises from the grave to prey on a group of teenagers stranded in the backwoods of Exeter.

According to folklore, a witch never dies. Neither, it appears, does Mercy Brown.

❧❦❧

REBECCA CORNELL: BURN, WITCH, BURN?

Hanged. Drowned. Beheaded. Burned. Such was the fate of many women accused and convicted of witchcraft the world over in the fifteenth, sixteenth and seventeenth centuries. Some, like Ireland's Bridget Cleary, met their demise at the hands of their own families. In 1894, Cleary was beaten and burned to death by family and friends, who believed she'd been spirited away by fairy folk and a witch left in her wake.

Lest Cleary's gruesome death be dismissed as anomaly, consider that it capped a misogynistic campaign of terror and cruelty lasting nearly three hundred years and spanning two continents. In death, Cleary joined a sorority numbering anywhere between ten thousand and sixty thousand women whom society deemed wicked.

Imagine the horror a woman felt when faced with such a fate. Now consider how acute her pain if it were family who put her in peril.

What Portsmouth's Rebecca Cornell felt in the last moments of her life is unknown. Like many women in her hometown of Essex, England, Cornell met a witch's fate: death by incineration. Unlike her Essex sisters, however, in her adopted country, Cornell was never charged or convicted of witchcraft in her lifetime. Her family members waited until Cornell was charred and cold before making the claim that she was a witch.

And, just maybe, they murdered her first.

Rebecca Cornell was a wealthy widow in the winter of her life when she died in February 1673. She was seventy-three, a property owner and matriarch of a large family. Cornell lived with her son Thomas, his second wife, Sarah, and their six children. Though the home the family lived in was large by colonial standards, Cornell had a large front room to herself while the rest of the family, a boarder and a servant shared what remained. Extant records of conversations produced at Cornell's murder trial indicate that Thomas and his mother fought over money. Thomas was indebted to his mother—dependent on her—a shameful position for a man of forty-six with a wife, six children and a seventh child on the way.

Cornell was keenly aware of her son's unhappiness. She confided to friend George Soule that she intended to leave her Portsmouth house for the home of another son if "shee was not otherwise disposed of, or made away," Soule said in a deposition quoted in Elaine Forman Crane's book, *Killed Strangely: The Death of Rebecca Cornell*. Such a statement indicates that Cornell did indeed fear for her life and that her end would come at the hand or hands of family members. Friends and neighbors recounted comments such as these when Cornell's son Thomas was tried, convicted and hanged for her murder in the spring of 1673. But the most damning testimony would come from Cornell herself—or, at least, her spirit—in a nocturnal visit to her brother, John Briggs, in the weeks after her death.

NOT A SCREAM SOUNDED

What is undisputed about Cornell's death on February 8, 1673, is that she was discovered lying in her bedroom, her corpse burnt "to a cole," Crane quotes. Son Thomas would argue that Cornell's death was likely due to her habit of smoking a pipe. He claimed that she set herself on fire after falling asleep with the lit pipe in her mouth. There were problems with Thomas's story. The most obvious was that a woman on fire would be likely to make some noise, and yet not a single member of the Cornell family noted hearing Cornell scream or even speak in the final hour or so of her life. Eight family members, a boarder and a servant dined on salted mackerel in the room next door, and no one heard a thing.

Not surprisingly, the community inquired as to the events preceding her death. Thomas said he was the last to see her alive. He'd gone into his mother's room after hearing that she was ill. There he found not only his mother, he said, but also his eldest son, his namesake. The younger Thomas left the room after his father entered. Son and mother remained in the room together for the space of about an hour and a half, Thomas said. When he left the room, Thomas had in his hand a quill around which he had begun winding yarn. He told his family that his mother would not be dining with them, as the meal, salted mackerel, was not to her liking.

It would be another forty-five minutes to an hour before anyone else entered Rebecca Cornell's room. At that point, Sarah sent her stepson, Edward, to Cornell's room with the instructions to ask the older woman whether she'd like some warm milk. According to Crane's research into the events of the evening, Edward Cornell, upon opening her door, called, "Grandmother, Grandmother!" and then ran in when he saw the woman aflame.

Cornell's body was buried two days later, on February 10, but her spirit was by no means at peace. On February 12, Cornell visited her brother, John Briggs, in a dream, charging him to "see how I was Burnt with fire," according to Briggs's testimony. The apparition must have been fearsome, as Briggs said it was burned from head to shoulders. What would have been dismissed as nightmare today was taken very seriously by the Quaker community in Portsmouth. Two weeks after her interment, Rebecca Cornell was exhumed and examined, and a new discovery was made that would be Thomas Cornell's undoing.

THE GHOST, THE GHOUL AND THE HELLHOUND

Quakers believed that dream visitations by ghosts were the work of one of two forces: God or the devil. If the spirit of a deceased person visited the living, it was believed that it was there at God's bidding to right a wrong. Unless, of course, the spirit was a sign of the devil's mischief, in which case such malevolence was easily enough rectified. A believer need only invoke the name of God when addressing the spirit, and it would be forced to flee, Quaker theology held. Briggs interpreted his visitation by Cornell as evidence of God's handiwork. He was moved to tell authorities of his vision in the week following his sister's burial. Others would follow, telling tales of Rebecca Cornell's fear of her son and his menacing nature.

When Rebecca Cornell's body was exhumed and her remains examined, doctors found that some object had punctured her in the vicinity of her stomach. Could it have been a wound inflicted by the spindle Thomas had in his hand when he withdrew from his mother's chamber, the spindle around which he had wound yarn? Why would the man have been doing such a thing? Wasn't that the chore of a woman? Such questions plagued at least one man involved in the inquiry. Crane notes that Richard Smith, in a letter to John Winthrop, the governor of Connecticut, wrote of the iron spindle Thomas had in his hand. Iron, it bears noting, was a metal abhorred by fairies and witches. Might Thomas have believed his mother to be supernatural? Evil, even?

Sarah Cornell took pains to establish this as fact. She insinuated that her mother-in-law was, indeed, a witch, a ghoul, who even had a familiar, a demon, in the form of a large black dog. No record of the Cornell's owning such a beast exists, and yet, Crane writes:

> When Edward opened his grandmother's door, "the Great Dogg being in her roome, Leaped out over the Boy." A dog vaulted over a standing teenager? Not likely. Some Rhode Islanders kept dogs in 1673, but no one had spoken of a family pet before, and even if none of the deponents had noticed it or thought the incident worth mentioning, it is puzzling that the family ignored what should have been a loudly barking canine in the next room. An ordinary dog crazed by smoke and flames would have created enough commotion to alert the family to some misfortune.

One would think so.

Sarah likely drew on her knowledge of folklore in creating this account of events. It was a well-established fact among colonial Anglo-Americans that witches had supernatural assistance in working their malevolent mischief. These people believed that demon helpers took the forms of cats, dogs or birds and were paid for their services by suckling the witch's blood. That is why women accused of witchcraft were subjected to the humiliation of being stripped naked and inspected. Inquisitors were looking for the witch's teat, the nipple or mole from which the demon drew sustenance.

Rebecca Cornell's hometown of Essex, a hotbed of witch-hunting activity, had in its folklore a demon dog called Black Shuck, which may have informed Sarah's tale. Black Shuck, Crane writes, "was as large as a calf with drooping ears, huge bright eyes, and a crimson tongue. These malevolent creatures were often associated with flame and fire." Crane further contends:

> Sarah Cornell's slyly disguised accusation of witchcraft insinuates that this great dog was really an imp or devil, a "familiar" long associated with witches in English popular thought. Indeed, the dog may have been Satan himself, whose presence at this catastrophic moment suggested that he had come to claim Rebecca's soul. Thomas's wife seems to have been implicating her mother-in-law in witchcraft.

Hardly the ideal mother-in-law/daughter-in-law relationship.

The Quaker community, though, took the word of a spirit over spiteful Sarah, and Thomas Cornell swung from the gallows of Miantonomi Hill on May 23. Sarah Cornell never veered from her claim of her husband's innocence. Later that year, Sarah gave birth to the couple's third daughter: Innocent.

Historians posit that women were killed for many reasons that had nothing to do with witchcraft. Old women were targets, as were women of diminished capacity. Cantankerous women were at risk, as were widowed women of some means. It is into the latter category that Portsmouth resident Rebecca Cornell falls. Rebecca Cornell was never, in her lifetime, charged or convicted of witchcraft, yet she endured a witch's fate. In her final moments, and posthumously, Rebecca Cornell suffered brutal assault to both body and reputation. And she was persecuted by those who should have loved her best: her family members.

⁂

THE DEVIL COMES A CALLIN'

The young women of Salem Village weren't the only New England girls to attempt to conjure the images of their future husbands. Westerly's Hannah Maxson and Comfort Cottrell sought supernatural intercession and nearly ended up with the devil himself for a mate.

During the Revolutionary War, Hannah and Comfort came to stay at the Westerly home of Esquire Clarke, recounts the Reverend S.S. Griswold in his *Historical Sketch of the Town of Hopkinton from 1757 to 1876*. The two girls were divining, seeking to learn whom their future husbands would be by performing a charm. They each threw a ball of yarn into a well and then wound it while repeating Scripture verses backward. In this way, they believed, they would reel in their future husbands like fish on a line.

What did they desire in their future helpmates? No doubt they wanted strong, handsome men capable of not only surviving but also thriving in the dark New England wood that was their new home. And wouldn't it be better if their husbands were also wealthy, powerful men of influence? To be the wife of such a man would make them the envy of all their friends. The idea was temptation enough to override any fears Hannah

and Comfort might have had about doing something so blasphemous as
saying Scripture backward.

They completed their ritual at dusk and then went indoors, waiting by the
home's entrance for the arrival of their beaux. Their incantations did their
work. A dark silhouette appeared on the horizon. No doubt the setting sun
made it difficult for the girls to see the figure clearly at first. Their girlish glee
at having successfully worked their charm soon turned to horror when they
saw that what strode toward them was no man but a hideous monster. It was
an eight- to ten-foot giant that came calling. The girls no doubt shuddered
at the fiend's enormous eyes the size of saucers and the flames that shot with
every breath from his bloated jaws. The husband come to claim his brides
was certainly not handsome. But he was capable. He wielded powerful
influence in their world, second only to God Himself.

Hannah Maxson and Comfort Cottrell had betrothed themselves to
Beelzebub. Their bridegroom was the devil.

The screams began when the creature turned from the street to the path
that led to the Clarke house. The girls ran to the room of the mistress of
the house, Mrs. Clarke, who lay sick in bed. Throwing themselves on the
poor woman, they must have made Mrs. Clarke sicker still to hear what
approached her home. Their ranting and raving also drew the home's other
occupant, Esquire Clarke, to his wife's room, no doubt in a rage at having
his wife's recuperation interrupted by two such vain and silly creatures. After
hearing the girls' wild story, Mr. Clarke went to meet the unwelcome visitor,
whose glaring eyes could be seen in the transom windows over the door.
Unfazed by the absolute certainty that a demon was on his doorstep, Esquire
Clarke met the monster head on. His weapon: prayer. The devil, incapable
of remaining in a place where God's name was invoked, fled, never to assert
his claim over the girls' souls again.

DOING BATTLE WITH THE DEVIL

The town of North Kingstown seems to have been a favorite haunt of
witches and ogres. Its swamps and desolate places were their preference,
argues Edgar Mayhew Bacon in his 1904 book, *Narragansett Bay:*

This ordinary street sign marks the site of an extraordinary battle between a witch and the devil himself. *Photo by M.E. Reilly-McGreen.*

Its Historic and Romantic Associations. "In North Kingstown," he writes, "witches abode, who held their unhallowed sabbaths in Hell Hollow and Kettle Hole."

North Kingstown holds the distinction of having the devil's own cloven footprint preserved for all eternity in a granite outcropping found just outside Wickford Village on Devil's Foot Road. Nearby, there is a second depression that looks very much like a human foot. The two petrosomatoglyphs, images of parts of human or animal bodies incised in rock, together mark the site of a fierce battle between the devil and one of his dark disciples.

The colonial-era legend tells of a Native American woman who sold her soul to Hobomock, the native people's name for Christianity's devil. In exchange, she received great power and plied her perverse talents in the caves in and about the area and perhaps as far north as Boston. When her contract with the devil came due, the woman was so practiced in her art that she thought to do battle with the devil to win back her soul. The squaw was also fleet of foot, and various legends tell of a footrace that extended from Boston to Wickford and Block Island before the woman met her end on the cliffs of Newport at a break in the rock aptly named Purgatory.

The Indian woman was apprehended by the devil after alighting on Devil's Foot Rock. Perhaps she meant to grab some charm or fetish to ward off the demon. The devil, however, took her and leapt across the Narragansett Bay to the cliffs of Newport. To still her struggling, the devil dashed her head several times on the rocks and finished his assault by chopping off her head with several strokes of his tomahawk. Some swings missed their intended mark, leaving impressions in the stone like the ones at Wickford. Legend says that the various depressions in the rocks at Purgatory mark the witch's bloody end. The "bowl-like depressions… where he bumped the squaw's head, the axe-marks where his tomahawk struck and the footprints in the vein of stone where he ran with the body of his victim up to the edge of Purgatory" are what remain of the epic battle, according to the July 30, 1916 *Providence Sunday Journal* article "Rhode Island Imprints of Beelzebub."

That's one way to lose your head over a guy.

❄

GRANNY MOTT: HOPKINTON'S HAG

The witches of the Brothers Grimm's world knew how to make mischief. Their potions turned princes to toads, and in their withered hands things as apparently benign as a simple spindle could render a princess catatonic for a century.

Folkloric witches' preferred method of torment was something known as hagging. Hagging, simply put, was the harassment of another to the point of vexation. Usually, the witch or hag would wait until night to attack. Her sleeping victim would awaken to find herself mute and paralyzed, barely able to breathe for the weight of the thing that squatted on her chest or squeezed her throat. Witch riding, as it was called, was the usual practice of the old hag; she sat on her victim and scared her silly in the process. There were those hags, however, who liked to get creative when it came to harassment.

Rhode Island's most famous old hag was Granny Mott of Hopkinton. In his *Historical Sketch of the Town of Hopkinton*, Reverend S.S. Griswold writes that Mott was of an advanced age in the 1740s and was known to be a witch by her neighbors. This did not appear to be a problem in the town, which was regarded by its inhabitants as a mecca for the magical world. Griswold writes:

> *Many houses in Hopkinton were haunted by spirits from the other world or the vasty [sic] deep, strange noises were heard, lights of various hues were seen, windows were illuminated, cannon balls were heard rolling across the floor, moaning cries were heard in the air, and many significant warnings of death were given; and maidens practiced various incantations in order to discover who their lovers and future husbands were to be.*

So there, Salem.

That Granny Mott distinguished herself in such a hotbed of paranormal activity as Hopkinton speaks to her influence. Granny Mott's powers were, if not formidable, then at least notable. Though she was not known to have been in possession of a magic broom, Granny Mott could get around more quickly than her fellow colonists. At that time, colonists often walked from one place to another in winter, not wanting to risk their horses twisting their legs on ice. Granny Mott, though, had no such concerns. "She could ride a smooth shod horse upon the ice at great speed," Griswold wrote.

Another curious habit of the hag was her ability to sit on sharp objects and show no pain. Granny Mott also distinguished herself in this arena. According to Griswold:

> *Mott once came to the house of Thomas Potter to procure work. Mr. Potter's son Stephen was playing about the floor when one of the older children whispered to him to stick an awl in the old woman's chair. She sat immovable for hours until the family became convinced she was a witch. Ever after when she visited the house she would stand, or sit upon a chest or bed, however many chairs might be near.*

She may have been able to show no pain, but it appears from Griswold's story that old Granny Mott likely felt it.

Legend has it that Granny Mott had one more talent: shape shifting. This is a witch's ability to change from human to animal form and back again. According to Griswold, Mott did just that to aggravate a neighboring farmer.

As the story goes, the farmer was under attack by a flock of heath hens. The boldest hen came at him directly, and despite firing at it repeatedly, the farmer could not kill it. The farmer then tore a silver button from his jacket, loaded his gun with it and shot and killed the bird. Griswold writes that the neighbor "soon heard that Granny Mott was sick unto death; and as her daughter who attended her refused all assistance in preparing the body for burial (for she died), it was believed that she was shot with the silver button in the person of that bird."

Why, of course, that makes perfect sense.

⊰⊱

NARRAGANSETT'S RUMPELSTILTSKIN

Stories of fairies and witches spinning flax and straw into gold are a common motif in many folkloric traditions. The Germans had Rumpelstiltskin, the Irish, Tom Tit Tot, and the Scotch dubbed their variant Whuppity Stoovie. Rhode Island's supernatural spinner was known simply as Narragansett's weaving witch.

Weaving was, for the most part, the domain of men, argues Alice Morse Earle in her 1898 collection of essays entitled *In Old Narragansett*. Though, she notes, "occasionally some sturdy woman, of masculine muscle and endurance, was a weaver."

The Narragansett weaving witch confounded her employers with her production of fine linen. No bride's hope chest was complete without one of her linen tablecloths, and many sought her shrouds to dress their dearly departed. Yet no one ever saw her produce any of these items. For hours on end, the witch would sit, silently staring at her loom, generating nothing.

Those around her would vent their anger to one another, but none directed a harsh word at the witch herself; they were too afraid of her wrath. Eventually, the witch would begin her work. Earle writes:

> *Suddenly she would sit up and start her treadle; bang! bang! would go her batten as fast as corn in a corn-popper; and at night, after she had gone home, when her piece was still set in the loom, the family would waken and hear the half-toned clapping of the loom, which someone*

The Narragansett Towers seem the perfect domicile for a wicked witch. *Author's collection.*

was running softly to help the witch out in her stint, probably the old black man.

The "old black man" is a common colonial euphemism for the devil.

At week's end, the witch would have more linen and carpet than any of her male co-workers. Earle notes that "whether it was hitching up with the devil or not, she always had employment in plenty."

What the witch didn't have were friends, aside from a cat that accompanied her to and from work. The witch kept to herself, electing not to eat or drink with her employers and coworkers, though that was the habit of all others employed at the mill. She also refused any drink, Earle says. "She never asked for water, nor cider, nor switchel, nor kill-devil."

There were whispers of familiars and shape shifting. One fellow weaver said that she saw a bumblebee fly out of the woman's mouth. In the same moment, a man in nearby Wickford who'd once quarreled with the witch was thrown from a horse after it had been stung on the nose by a bumblebee. Of course, the two events were linked, the gossips said. Still, no one dared accuse the old woman of witchcraft. Perhaps the weaving witch's co-workers and neighbors may have been motivated by something other than fear. Some members of the community certainly had other selfish reasons for overlooking her idiosyncrasies. The woman's own brand of witches brew, metheglin, commonly known as mead, was prized in Old Narragansett. It seems that a few stories of spells and some minor mischief were not reason enough to separate a man from his mead.

DEVIL'S HANDMAIDEN OR A FELINE'S BEST FRIEND?

Another incident that raised suspicion involved the weaving witch's cat. A kitchen fire broke out in the building where the witch worked. The inhabitants of the house ran from the fearsome flames, but none thought or cared to alert the old woman working in the loom loft. Earle notes:

> The bang and rattle of her work made [the witch] ignorant of the noise and commotion below, and as the smoke entered the loft she thought, "But that chimney do smoke!" Finally a conviction of danger came to her and she made her way down the loft-ladder and through the entry with difficulty to the open air.

The witch no doubt looked with scorn and contempt at the shamefaced crew that had left her to die in the loom loft. Her only remark, however, was to enquire after her cat. Upon learning that the animal was likely still inside the burning house, she braved smoke and flame to save it. When she came out again, the cat was cradled in her arms. Witnesses speculated that her concern for the animal was not that of owner for pet but of witch for demon familiar.

Still, the woman was left alone to go about her business. The last story Earle recounts is of the witch in the final days of her solitary life. A neighbor encountered the old woman on the road home to her hovel. He told his wife that the witch was holding her side, her breathing was labored and her pace was slow. Word spread to the town's minister, who pronounced her failing health evidence of God's displeasure with her. One woman the minister visited in his rounds heard him wax on about the witch getting her due and decided to look in on the wretched creature. The woman arrived to find the witch dead in a cold and cheerless hovel.

Sometime later, a group of boys paid a visit to the old woman's house. With the invention of spray paint still far off in the future, the boys vandalized the hovel as best they could, breaking windows and wrenching open the front door. The sight that greeted them when they entered the hut stopped them cold, though. The sack of mouse barley that had been the witch's bed had sprouted, covering her final resting place, Earle writes, in a carpet as verdant and green as the one that graced her grave.

In "Rumpelstiltskin" and other stories like it, the plot is fairly predictable. A young maiden is given an insurmountable task: to turn flax or straw into gold in the space of a day or face certain death. When the witch or fairy arrives on the scene, the young girl bargains away her soul or that of her firstborn child for the creature's supernatural services. The pact is made but not without an escape clause for the girl. If she can learn the name of the malevolent creature, she is free of her obligation. Folklorists note that the gullible devil is always thwarted in such stories and is forced to leave infuriated and empty-handed.

Like the maiden in "Rumpelstiltskin," the enterprising soul may have profited had she discovered the true name of the Narragansett weaving witch.

Alas, it appears no one bothered.

ELIZABETH SEAGER: THE DEVIL AS HER WITNESS?

Was Elizabeth Seager the black-hearted, evil hag her neighbors suspected her to be?

A convicted blasphemer and an adulterer, Seager was unpleasant and given to melodrama, that much is true. But was she a witch? Did Goodwife Seager dance with the Prince of Darkness by moonlight and cast spells on her God-fearing neighbors by day?

Well, Seager didn't quite deny it. In fact, when asked if she were a witch, she said she'd call upon the devil himself to prove otherwise.

It seems Seager failed to see that Satan, aka the "Father of Lies," might prove a problematic witness for the defense. At least, for most people.

By broom or foot, Elizabeth Seager fled her Hartford, Connecticut home for Rhode Island about 1665, sometime after her third trial for witchcraft. The number three proved quite unlucky for the woman. She was convicted and sentenced to be hanged. When a technicality resulted in her verdict being set aside, Goody Seager bid Connecticut farewell.

What horrors had she committed? What black magic had she worked? Well, her neighbor, Goodwife Margaret Garrett, charged her with bewitching a block of cheese. Garrett said she suspected that Seager was the cause of half a block of her cheese being maggot-ridden. Garrett testified in court that she had her proof when, after throwing the maggot-ridden cheese into the fire, Goody Seager, working nearby, screamed in pain. Ridiculous? Not to a society that believed in a World of Wonders, where the supernatural explanation was completely, well, natural. Remember, this is the same society whose members believed they could undo a witch's spell if they boiled her blood or urine. In the absence of readily available bodily fluids, another way to thwart a witch was to burn the object of her magic.

Like a block of cheese, for example.

AN UNWANTED WOMAN

Clearly, Seager's accusers thought her a malignancy that had to be excised, notes author John Taylor in his book *The Witchcraft Delusion in Colonial Connecticut (1647–1697)*. Taylor suspects that she was a woman deserving of her fate:

> *Goody Seager probably deserved all that came to her in trials and punishment. She was one of the typical characters in the early communities upon whom distrust and dislike and suspicion inevitably fell. Exercising witch powers was one of her more reputable qualities. She was indicted for blasphemy, adultery, and witchcraft at various times, was convicted of adultery, and found guilty of witchcraft in June, 1665. She owed her escape from hanging to a finding of the Court of Assistants that the jury's verdict did not legally answer to the indictment, and she was set "free from further suffering or imprisonment."*

In her final trial, half of the jurors believed Seager guilty of the charges leveled against her. And it is likely that even those who were inclined to believe Seager innocent would have had their misgivings about the woman. Why? The most damning testimony against Seager was her own words. To her accusers, she offered the most remarkable of alibis, as related by Goodwife Margaret Garrett and reproduced here exactly as entered into court record:

This deponent after she had a little paused said, who did you say, then good Seger sd againe she had sent Satan to tell them she was no witch. This deponent asked her why she made use of Satan to tell them, why she did not besech God to tell them she was no witch. She answered because Satan knew she was no witch.

Historian Richard Godbeer, in his book *Escaping Salem: The Other Witch Hunt of 1692*, writes that the community was infuriated to see Seager escape the noose. To put it in terms the contemporary person would understand, it was akin to releasing a career criminal back into the community. It didn't matter that Elizabeth Seager's great crime was cheese spoilage. She was the embodiment of evil incarnate to her community. Allowing Seager to live, her neighbors felt, was to put all others' safety in jeopardy. And their anger was righteous, sanctioned by God Himself. Exodus 22:18 commands, "Thou shalt not suffer a witch to live."

To what Rhode Island town or hamlet Seager retired is not known. Journalist Charles J. Hoadly, in an 1899 *Connecticut Magazine* article entitled "A Case of Witchcraft in Hartford," says of Seager, "After about a year's imprisonment she was released and found Rhode Island a more congenial place of residence." One legend holds that she took up residence in Richmond.

To date, no printed account of further malevolence toward neighbors or cheese has yet been found.

THE SPANISH SEA WITCH

Fortune does not smile on the Spanish lady in literature. Though much is made of her grace and beauty, these very things work against her when in the hands of the storyteller. She is plundered and brutalized, a prize to be had for the taking by unscrupulous men.

Take the legend of Narragansett's Donna Mercedes Wedderburn, for instance. This sad lass was allegedly murdered and walled up in her seaside mansion by her tyrannical husband, a sea captain. The ill-fated Mrs. Wedderburn's story could have been the inspiration for poet Walt Whitman's

"The Spanish Lady." In his version, the Lady Inez is moments away from the unwanted attention of marauders. He writes:

> *O, better had she laid here*
> *Mid the couches of the dead;*
> *O better had she slumbered*
> *Where the poisonous snake lay hid.*
>
> *For worse than deadly serpent,*
> *Or moldering skeleton,*
> *Are the fierce bloody hands of men,*
> *By hate and fear urged on.*
>
> *O Lady Inez, pleasant*
> *Be the thoughts that now have birth*
> *In thy visions; they are last of all*
> *That thou shalt dream on earth.*

Theft, rape and death—such is the fate of the Spanish lady in literature. Need another example? Consider the Spanish lady who figures so prominently in yet another Block Island wrecker tale immortalized in Charles Dana's poem "The Buccaneer" and in Edgar Mayhew Bacon's *Narragansett Bay: Its Historic and Romantic Associations*. These recount the story of the Block Island wrecker and pirate Captain Lee, who agrees to take a beautiful Spanish widow, her servants and her white palfrey, a horse, aboard his ship. The exotic woman's wealth and beauty prove equal lures for Lee, a man of little kindness and no mercy. Once Lee's ship is put to sea, the nefarious captain and his crew feed the widow's servants to the sharks, leaving the woman alone with the men.

The widow, no doubt realizing that her fate would be rape and then murder, chose instead to fling herself into the sea. Captain Lee was incensed at being cheated out of his prize and, in a rage, ordered that the woman's snow-white palfrey join its virtuous mistress:

> *For a while the crew amused themselves by watching the creature's efforts to swim after the ship, but at last, with a great cry, it sank. Then Lee turned to his cabin, sullen and silent. His men feared him, telling each other that he had the evil eye; one of them he stabbed in a drunken fury and threw his body overboard, and his ruffians crossed themselves,*

being sure that the shriek they heard was nothing less than the neigh of the white horse.

Captain Lee and his crew continued their misadventures for some time but eventually returned to Block Island. Their intent was to live ashore for a spell, enjoying their ill-gotten gains. And so they did, until one night when a fiery spectacle drew them down to the island's rocky shores. Lee and his men watched, paralyzed with horror, as the spectral wreck that advanced toward them bore on it all of their victims. There was the crew member Lee had tossed overboard and the Spanish lady's servants. At the forefront of this macabre crew of the undead was the Spanish-lady-turned-sea-witch, "whose veil floated like a pall upon the blood-red waters." And leading the charge was the white palfrey, swimming ably toward Lee. When it came ashore, the evil man mounted it and was spirited off to the sea. Like the Celtic kelpie, this spectral steed appeared to have the power to compel Lee to mount it and bear him away.

Legends differ on the fate of the man who mounts a spectral steed. If the Spanish palfrey followed the instincts of its Celtic cousin, it would have drowned and then eaten the wicked captain. Another story holds, though, that the rider is damned to stay atop the steed for all eternity, never stopping, never resting. Those who would tell the story of Block Island's brutal buccaneer stop short of speculating further. Suffice it to say, though, the lascivious Lee met his match in the Spanish widow and her white steed.

⚜

TALL "DUTCH" KATTERN: MYSTIC OR MENACE?

What caused the crew of the ill-fated ship the *Palatine* to strand sorceress Tall "Dutch" Kattern on Block Island? Could it be that a group of salty sea dogs feared the wrath of a single woman?

One legend holds that they were right to worry. In it, the oft-reviled castaway, Tall "Dutch" Kattern, known to her neighbors alternately as an opium eater, soothsayer and witch, is the wicked woman whose thirst for vengeance caused the ship to run aground and catch fire.

Thirteen Witches and a Vampire

A postcard of a ship wrecked on the coast of Block Island. *Author's collection.*

The facts underpinning the *Palatine* legend are these: On December 26, 1738, the *Princess Augusta*, subsequently dubbed the *Palatine* for its passengers, German Palatines, found itself in stormy, frigid seas. It had been a harrowing voyage for passengers and crew alike. Disease had decimated those on board. Their number had dwindled to half of what it was when the Palatines boarded the ship in Rotterdam, writes Michael Bell in his article "The Legend of the *Palatine*." Rough seas ran the ship aground at Block Island's Sandy Point. Once crew and passengers had disembarked, the ship was set adrift and smashed to pieces when it ran into rocks.

The passengers, many sickly, were taken in by the islanders and nursed to health. Those who did not survive were buried in a mass grave, now graced with a stone marker, into which is chiseled "Palatine Graves 1738."

Where fact ends, fancy flourishes.

There is the tale that one passenger, a woman, would not leave the ship and met her death on board after it was lured to the island, looted and set afire by marauding islanders, also known as wreckers. Then there is the story that the *Palatine* still haunts Block Island's shores in the form of a spectral ship, the *Palatine Light*, which may be seen on the horizon between Christmas and New Year's Eve. Poet John Greenleaf Whittier spun a similar yarn in his 1867 poem "The *Palatine*":

The site of the wreck of the *Princess Augusta*, immortalized by John Greenleaf Whittier in his poem "The *Palatine*." *Photo by James Manni.*

> *The eager islanders one by one*
> *Counted the shots of her signal gun,*
> *And heard the crash when she drove right on!*
>
> *Into the teeth of death she sped:*
> *(May God forgive the hands that fed*
> *The false lights over the rocky Head!)*

Whittier's Palatines pray for deliverance, but the islanders prove more malignant than the stormy seas. He writes:

> *Down swooped the wreckers, like birds of prey*
> *Tearing the heart of the ship away,*
> *And the dead had never a word to say.*
>
> *And then, with ghastly shimmer and shine*
> *Over the rocks and the seething brine*
> *They burned the wreck of the* Palatine.

Or did they? Might Whittier have gotten it wrong?

The Old Harbor View Hotel on Block Island employed at least one ancestor of Tall "Dutch" Kattern. *Author's collection.*

S.T. Livermore, in his *A History of Block Island from Its Discovery in 1514, to the Present Time, 1876*, writes of the *Palatine*'s passenger Tall "Dutch" Kattern's role in the demise of the ship. With obvious scorn, he recounts one island legend in which "the superstitions, and fictitious relations of said ship and light originated in the days of the witch, 'Dutch Kattern,'" the inveterate "opium eater," who along with another islander, "the maniac, Mark Dodge, are poor authority for authenticating a legend that criminates a civil, Christianized community." Livermore rants further that "the representing of an entire community of law-abiding Christian people as barbarians and pirates, and that too, on the testimony of a witch, an opium-eater and a maniac, is intolerable."

Wicked witch or inveterate liar, Dutch Kattern did claim responsibility for the tragedy, according to Livermore. He writes that the "low-bred 'Dutch Kattern'...had her revenge on the ship that put her ashore by imagining it on fire, and telling others, probably, that the light on the sound was the wicked ship *Palatine* cursed for leaving her on Block Island."

Dutch Kattern also claimed to be able to foretell the future. And though there is no evidence of her having a familiar, she is linked to a haunted house on the island, which had, among its contents, a dancing mortar. This heavy wooden bowl, used for grinding grain into flour, was hewn from salvaged

The Palatine Graves monument commemorates the lives of those lost in the wreck of the *Princess Augusta* in 1738. *Photo by James Manni.*

timber of the accursed *Palatine*. Legend says it had the ability to move of its own accord and was only stilled when pinned by large boulders. The owner of the home, Livermore's aforementioned maniacal Mark Dodge, likely spread the story of the mortar, as he was credited with telling many stories of being haunted by his home's previous tenants.

Dutch Kattern married a freed slave and remained on Block Island for the rest of her life. Sort of.

Kattern is said to have claimed to be able to separate her spirit from her body for brief sojourns overseas. She would go into a trance, according to island folklore, thereby allowing her spirit to leave her body, travel to her homeland and reconnect with the family she left behind.

No doubt some islanders vainly wished that where her spirit went her body would follow.

Sylvia Tory:
Witch of Ministerial Woods

Folklore holds that there are certain accoutrements, or tools of the trade, ascribed to witches. They have grimoires, or books of spells, which they consult when whipping up a love potion or working on a hex. Witches might also have poppets, little dolls made in enemies' likenesses, upon which they would work their spells or inflict terrible pain with the prick of a pin. Finally, there were familiars, demons who assumed animal shapes, suckled by witches in exchange for assistance in the black arts.

Sylvia Tory needed no such assistance in her soothsaying, or so extant records would have us believe. Unlike other alleged Rhode Island witches, like her contemporary Tuggie Bannock, Sylvia Tory proved herself to be in possession of some potent powers on at least one occasion. Unfortunately, Tory's success signaled another's demise. In this terrible tale, death was very nearly purchased for the price of a quarter.

Tory was likely African American, the freed slave of Matthew Robinson, a prominent local lawyer who, in his will, freed her in 1795. She is believed to have been married to fellow slave Cuff Tory, whom she likely met at Hopewell, Robinson's estate, west of the Kingston Railroad Station, according to a *Providence Journal* newspaper article entitled "Sylvia Tory, Known as the Witch of South Kingstown."

Tory held a certain fascination for another powerful local family, the Hazards, Peace Dale mill owners. One, Thomas Robinson Hazard, writes a lengthy account of an encounter with the witch of Ministerial Road in his book, coauthored with Rowland Gibson Hazard, called *The Jonnycake Papers of Shepherd Tom: Together with Reminiscences of Narragansett Schools of Former Days (1915)*.

What is interesting about Hazard is his belief in Tory's powers despite his being of a decidedly skeptical nature, as displayed in his account of running a Doctor Sangrado, "a Connecticut human blood–swilling allopath," and others of his "hell-born profession" out of town. Hazard writes that Sangrado was employed to try to rid the area of the "dusty death," or typhus, "a fatal malady," which

> was altogether caused by the malpractice of Sangrado and his bleeding compeers, upon which discovery Sangrado was forced by the public indignation to leave Narragansett and flee back to Connecticut (the Devil's

South Kingstown sibyl Sylvia Tory made her home in Ministerial Woods. The rhododendron- and mountain laurel–lined road traversing the woods has been designated one of the state's scenic streets. *Photo by M.E. Reilly-McGreen.*

own state), where he succeeded in making a meager living by persuading enough priest and doctor ridden patients to consent to be sent their graves through his administering…doses of soothing but life-destroying morphine, opiates, and other mineral compounds and drugs.

Hazard has no such vitriol for Tory. In fact, he seems to hold her in esteem. Hazard casts Tory as an old-school witch; wizened and old, she scratches a scant living soothsaying from her hovel tethered in the verdant tangle of rhododendrons and mountain laurel of "Ministerial Woods," which lie a "half mile south and west of the Tom Rodman corner, and beyond Sot's Hole" and extend through "Hardscrabble to Tuckertown." Whether by nature or design, Tory is given to delivering cryptic messages and ominous warnings of impending doom. What she is not inclined to do is take money from a soon-to-be dead man. Hazard laps it up like a cat would cream:

In a small hovel way off in the north-west corner of the forest, lived the old black sibyl or fortune-teller or prophetess or spirit-medium or witch, just as one's fancy might call her (they being all the same), Sylvia Tory, who died at the age of one hundred and four years, who Adam Babcock and Charles Barker (journeyman apprentice to Jonathan N. Hazard, carpenter), together with myself, went some miles one Sunday afternoon (about the year eighteen hundred and twenty) to see, and get "Sylvy Tory" to tell our fortunes (all entire strangers to her), which she did for Charles and me, dwelling upon our future life for an hour or so more in truth than fiction, so far as I at least was concerned, but when she came to Adam Babcock (then in robust health), not a word could he get from the old shriveled, gray-headed crone save, "Don't you by no means go east," which Sylvia repeated so often as Adam pressed her to say more, for some half a dozen times, without a word's addition or subtraction, "Don't you by no means go east!" which made Adam mad, but still he offered to pay her his quarter, the same as we did, which she persistently refused to accept, and on my asking the contrary old critter after Adam had gone outdoors, why she would not tell him his fortune, the old witch shook her head oracularly and said that "that young fellow has no fortune to tell"; and sure enough, when Adam's indentures had expired, a week later, he went straight to New Bedford, some thirty miles due east of Sylvia's hovel, where he sickened in a few days and died a fortnight later.

Hazard places Tory among the ranks of other local witches, characterizing her as slightly less powerful than Rhode Island mystic Jemima Wilkinson, "the greatest sibyl or spirit medium in America," but on par with "Old Stover, of Tiverton," the witches and wizards "that were drowned and pressed to death in Salem" and "the four Quakers who were hung by the wicked Puritans on Boston Common."

Descendant Caroline Hazard also appears spellbound by Tory. In her collection of poems entitled *Narragansett Ballads*, she pays tribute to Tory in the poem "The Fortune Teller." The ballad tells of a young girl who braves the dark woods to ask Tory if her lover, a sailor, will soon return to her. Hazard writes:

Deep in the wood an old crone dwells,
An aged dame so hoary,
And all the future she foretells,
The wise old Sylvia Tory.
And to her hut at fall of night
Comes many an anxious maiden,

And many a youth in sorry plight,
To ease their hearts love-laden.

The girl is beside herself. She tells the clairvoyant that she's dreamt of her lover's demise. Tory seeks to pacify her, saying:

Now, peace, my child, and say no word;
Thy dreams may truly frighten.
I'll listen well; then what I've heard
I'll tell, thy fears to lighten.

Tory tells the girl that, though the boy faced a battle at sea, he survived to enjoy the glory and spoils of victory. She instructs the girl:

Go to the sea, thou maiden fair,
With father and with brother;
Thy true love surely will be there
In two days and another.

The lovers reunite at the poem's end, and the maiden states her intention to return to Tory, saying, "Old Sylvia here will have good cheer / To find thee home already."

Sylvia Tory went by many names—spirit-medium, sibyl, prophetess and witch—but to those who knew her, it seems it was her sterling character that made her most memorable.

Jemima Wilkinson: Holy Woman or Heretic?

Jemima Wilkinson claimed to be able to walk on water and resurrect the dead. When her claims were tested, Wilkinson's boasts cost her, to be sure, but the men in her life may have paid a dearer price. For when Jemima Wilkinson came calling, men's reputations and cash reserves had a habit of disappearing.

Thirteen Witches and a Vampire

Wilkinson was born in Cumberland in 1752, the eighth of twelve children. Writers have described Wilkinson as a great beauty who spurned the advances of all eligible men her age. Her passion was reserved for prayer and contemplation. In 1776, at the age of twenty-four, Wilkinson fell ill with fever. This would prove to be the seminal event in the young woman's life. When Wilkinson awoke from her fever, she claimed to have risen from the dead and to have had a vision of angels telling her to preach. And for the next forty years, she did.

But not without controversy. Before her death in 1819 at the age of sixty-seven, Wilkinson would be called a fraud, a heretic, a witch and a whore. She seems not to have suffered any self-esteem issues, however. In fact, some writers and historians suggest that Wilkinson may even have thought herself to be the second coming of the Messiah.

Wilkinson merited more than a mention in Salem jail keeper Robert Ellis Cahill's book *New England's Witches and Wizards*. In his essay about her, called "Rhode Island's Pretty Mystic," Cahill characterizers her as a willful, spoiled girl given to theatrics. He writes:

> *She was, by far, the most beautiful of the Wilkinson children, and she thrived on the attention little boys and cooing adults would give her. She disliked anything that would make her dirty, and thus she shirked all housework, usually faining* [sic] *some kind of illness.*

When Wilkinson reached her mid-twenties, she found that men's interest in her had begun to wane. Ellis suggests that it was this realization that caused her to take to her bed for two years, during which time the prodigious fever and vision took place. In her article "'Resurrection' Inspired Her to Preach," *Providence Journal* reporter Maria Miro Johnson contends that Wilkinson believed that, like Jesus Christ and Lazarus before him, she had died and been resurrected.

Edgar Mayhew Bacon, in his 1904 book *Narragansett Bay: Its Historic and Romantic Associations*, writes of the would-be miracle worker's claims of resurrection, saying:

> *She was dead and her spirit had departed—but the reincarnated spirit of the Saviour of Mankind animated her restored body. This blasphemous assumption was coupled with the statement that in this form He would dwell upon earth and reign a thousand years.*

When she revived, Wilkinson changed her name to "Publick Universal Friend" and told family and friends that the angels had told her it was her duty to perform miraculous deeds for the good of humanity. A local minister encouraged Wilkinson to speak of her experience.

Ellis set the scene:

> At the church meeting, the seemingly shy, beautiful young lady, with long flowing strawberry-blonde hair, was called to the pulpit. She began by telling the congregation of how she had gone into a trance for three days, during which time she had had many visions. One spirit, she said, told her that she would live for 1,000 years, and another revealed that she would become the leader of spiritual affairs in America.

The audience was entranced. Wilkinson began speaking with greater frequency, and her influence expanded to other Rhode Island communities. And as her popularity grew, so did her ego. She began making claims of having magical powers. Ellis writes:

> At East Greenwich, she stated to a gathering of 35 people, "one of you within the sound of my voice will not live another day." That night, a black servant boy who had heard Jemima speak doubled up in pain and dropped dead. Although a neighbor was accused of poisoning the boy, Jemima got all the credit.

One of Wilkinson's most outrageous claims was that she, like Jesus Christ, would walk on water. She chose Swansea, Massachusetts, and Mount Hope Bay as the venue for her miracle moment. Thousands turned out to see this feat. When the comely preacher found herself wading rather than walking on water, the crowd turned on her. They laughed and jeered, Ellis writes. In turn, he says, "she called them all 'servants of the Devil' and 'disbelievers.'" She then returned with her remaining followers to Rhode Island.

Public humiliation did not cause Wilkinson to question her alleged supernatural abilities or have doubts about her destiny, however. Perhaps the young preacher's greatest gift was her power of persuasion. She had meetinghouses built for her in two communities, and at least one man was willing to part with wealth and reputation for her. Judge William Potter of Kingston, Rhode Island, built a fourteen-room addition onto his mansion as headquarters for Wilkinson and her followers, the Jemimakins. In return, legend has it, Wilkinson was to cure his gravely ill daughter. She failed, and

---

the little girl died. Wilkinson then promised to bring Potter's daughter back from the dead. Strike two. Whether it was that or the thousands of dollars Wilkinson had siphoned off of Potter that finally caused the break between the preacher and the judge is unclear, but the relationship ended.

Johnson suggests another factor in the demise of the friendship: Mrs. Potter. One account holds that the judge would often visit Wilkinson alone in her private rooms off his house. Mrs. Potter is said to have interrupted one such session. Ever the preacher, Wilkinson defended her part in the liaison, saying that "she was only ministering to one of her lambs, whereupon Mrs. Potter is said to have retorted: 'Minister to your lambs all you want, but in the future please leave my old ram alone,'" Johnson writes.

Bacon adds that the

> *chicanery and subterfuges which she employed in working her pretended miracles preclude the theory that she was self-deceived. Her moral character was notoriously bad, and at one time a robbery of public money was traced to her, but so strong was her influence that she escaped punishment.*

The robbery of public money may refer to the story of an overnight visit Wilkinson allegedly paid to Rhode Island's state treasurer's home. When the treasurer awoke in the morning, he found Wilkinson and her followers gone, along with several thousand dollars of taxpayer money. When law enforcement officials caught up with Wilkinson later, she was carrying a suitcase containing $800, Ellis reports. She was likely unapologetic, if Ellis is to be believed:

> *Jemima rode a white stallion as she traveled from town to town preaching and predicting. She also wore a long woolen cape, literally pulling the wool over the eyes of skeptics who confronted her. She was not only beautiful but gained the reputation of a "spitfire," who would just as soon strike a man or woman down as to look at them.*

This from a woman preaching a philosophy underpinned by adherence to nonviolence and the Golden Rule.

Wilkinson and her Jemimakins made their final home in upstate New York. She purchased a large piece of land, perhaps with the unrecovered cash from Rhode Island's state coffers, and built a farm there. Wilkinson dubbed her home Little Jerusalem and lived there with fifty followers. Sect members, legend says, could not be too pretty or they would be banished.

Wilkinson's ability to foretell the future failed her again in old age. Ellis notes that the would-be Messiah died more than nine centuries short of her promised one thousand years.

Perhaps two resurrections in one lifetime are just too much to expect.

⁂

The Witch of Hopkins Hill

Kent County's Hopkins Hill Summit rises 495 feet above sea level and surveys Arcadia, a stunning vista of pastoral beauty in the Ocean State. Those who live in the vicinity of the mountain summit no doubt know better than most the allure of such a place. As do witches. Hopkins Hill Summit was once prime real estate for witches looking to do a little magic and, sometimes, a bit of mischief.

The summit was the home of one of the area's most nefarious witches, says Edgar Mayhew Bacon in *Narragansett Bay: Its Historic and Romantic Associations*. He writes:

> *There is an acclivity known as Hopkins Hill, once the scene of many a witches' frolic. A boulder in a nearby wood bears the ominous name of Witches Rock, and marks a spot where in a wretched hovel one of the most dreaded of the evil sisterhood brewed her philters and worked her unhallowed charms.*

The Witches Rock was not prized by anyone but the witch, it seemed. Covered in poison ivy, sumac and deadly nightshade, it was the bane of one farmer, a man named Reynolds, who swore to remove the rock with his plow. Whether it was the man's boast or the rock's evil purpose that drew the crowd to witness Reynolds's feat that day is a mystery. Perhaps those gathered knew that the rock would not be removed without a fight. Mayhew thinks so:

> *As every one knows—every one that is, who is versed in occult lore—there is a deadly animosity between witches and ploughshares, as between witches and horse-shoes, possibly because of an early fashion of heating the iron*

48

red-hot and making one suspected of witchcraft walk barefooted upon it.
If the victim's feet were not burned she was a witch. If they were, she was
simply unfortunate.

So true.

Mr. Reynolds's efforts were not rewarded. Three times he tried to unearth
the rock, and three times he failed. His ox yoke broke, and his oxen's legs
buckled under the strain. The battle for dominion over the rock was just
getting started, however.

First, a big, black crow flew from the forest to perch on the branch of
a dead tree and proceeded to caw its displeasure at the seething farmer.
The farmer shouted at the bird words that seemed to work a spell on the
bird. The bird fell from the branch onto the boulder, and a pin, part of
the ox yoke, fell from its beak. The crowd barely had time to register its
surprise at the farmer's power before the bird transformed into the evil
witch who haunted Hopkins Hill. There was no mistaking who she was as
she had in hand her besom broom of nettlestalks and her "bell-crowned
hat," Mayhew notes.

Frightened, Reynolds and the crowd reared back as the raging witch
changed shape yet again. This time, she took the form of a large black
cat, which leapt from the boulder and disappeared into a crevice at its
base. The crowd joined Reynolds in a vain attempt to dig it out. Despair
soon set in, and the crowd began to disperse. Reynolds struck the rock
with his broken ploughshare with such great force that it dented the
rock. But the dent was all the damage Mr. Reynolds managed to inflict
that day.

The witch had won.

⊰⊱

WITCHES' ALTAR

Once, a visit to Narragansett's Witches' Altar was a rite of passage, a
measure of a teenager's mettle. Past the lush emerald lawns of gorgeous
Stanford White–style summer cottages, the altar crouched, choked by
brambles, cloaked in the detritus of years of unchecked weedy growth. Like

Hazard Castle, home of spiritualist Joseph Peace Hazard and his fairy folk. *Author's collection.*

Kendall Green has come to be better known as Witches' Altar. *Photo by M.E. Reilly-McGreen.*

Joseph Peace Hazard. *Photo courtesy of the Peace Dale Library's Special Collections.*

something out of a fairy tale, it lay in wait, in the wild wood beyond the shingled castles that lined Gibson Avenue. The intrepid explorer could not expect to escape the wood without sacrificing arms and legs to the teeth of thorns and, perhaps, an evil case of poison ivy or sumac.

That is, if she returned at all.

Legend has it that the circle of eight granite pillars was the site of all sorts of wicked enterprises. Some said this was the place of witches' midnight meetings, where they and their familiars would dance by the light of the full moon. Other stories held that this was the scene of witches' executions, a gallows of sorts, haunted still by the spirits of those sacrificed to appease a community's fears.

None of this was true, of course. Witches and familiars? Hardly. Joseph Peace Hazard wasn't after witches when he built what would become Witches' Altar. He wanted Druids.

Hazard, a member of one of South County's wealthiest and most successful families, built Kendall Green, aka Witches' Altar, as an antemortem memorial for himself, his family members and a few close friends. At one time, the four-foot granite pillars encircled a thirteen-foot granite obelisk imprinted, in part, with the following: "JOSEPH PEACE HAZARD of the CASTLE

Druid's Dream. *Photo by M.E. Reilly-McGreen.*

AT SEA SIDE, R.I." All that remains of the centerpiece today is a rough-hewn, crumbling base.

Hazard, a spiritualist, was a quiet bachelor who managed, in spite of himself, to attract attention for his esoteric proclivities. An 1889 *Providence Journal* article about his obelisk, reprinted in the *New York Times*, attests to as much:

Thirteen Witches and a Vampire

Mr. Joseph Peace Hazard has recently erected another granite pillar on "Kendall Green," the well-known memorial plot of ground off the Point Judith road, at Narragansett Pier. The pillar was built by R.A. Harrall of Wakefield, and stands at the corner of Hazard and Gibson avenues, west of "Druid's Dream," the stone building.

The cut stone, gabled Druid's Dream, a twenty-one-room house, was inspired, so the story goes, by a dream Hazard had. Hazard told friends that he built the structure because he dreamed an ancient Celtic Druid demanded that he do so. Hazard, a world-traveled spiritualist who believed that communion between the living and the dead was possible, never lived in the house, presumably because he wanted it always at the ready for his intended guest.

Hazard lived in nearby Hazard Castle. There, according to legend, Hazard had installed screened niches, into which he put offerings of food for the spirits with whom he shared his home. Hazard's devotion did not end with the niches, however. Sometime during the 1880s, Hazard commissioned a 105-foot tower to be added to his Norman-style home. Called Hazard's Folly by some, the massive structure was completed in 1883. The tower was a grand gesture, a testament to Hazard's spiritual beliefs, as he thought it would bring him closer to his beloved spirit world. A second tower was planned for Tower Hill, but it never materialized. In 2009, Hazard's Castle was offered for sale at an asking price of $7 million.

Hazard's creations have generated their fair share of eerie tales. Most of the haunting thereabouts nowadays is done by teenagers and thrill-seekers. Some are likely disappointed to find the Witches' Altar cleared of brambles and brush, demarcated by the telltale white metal sign that humbly identifies it as just one of the state's three thousand historical cemeteries.

But certainly that's enough to scare away any privacy-seeking witches or Druids.

PART II

WENCHES OR WRETCHES?

BETSY BOWEN:
"VICE-QUEEN OF AMERICA"

Eliza "Betsy" Bowen de la Croix Brown Jumel Burr had a name so lengthy that it rivaled that of the most titled member of the aristocracy and a personal fortune that likely exceeded that of most nobility. And that name carried with it a story of sex, lies, larceny and insanity that rivaled the plot of the wildest romance novel.

Betsy Bowen was born in Providence in 1775, the bastard child of Phebe Kelley and John Bowen, a prostitute and a sailor, respectively. She was the third child of the dissolute pair, whose lifestyle often put the two in conflict with the Providence Town Council. Phebe, in particular, was often called before the town fathers on charges of vagrancy and prostitution. After the death of her husband and her marriage to another, John Clarke, Phebe was thrown out of Providence for good, banished once more for vagrancy.

Phebe's two eldest daughters, Betsy and Polly, likely spent at least part of their childhood in houses of ill repute and the rest in the homes of the various men Phebe attached herself to in between husbands. The Bowen girls, of course, had no formal education. Nor were they likely schooled in the domestic arts of sewing and cooking. But what they did learn under their

A picture postcard of the Jumel Mansion. *Author's collection.*

mother's tutelage was how to survive in a man's world. And so, when their mother and stepfather left Providence for Massachusetts in 1790, the girls remained in Providence. The period of apprenticeship was over. In his 1916 book entitled *The Jumel Mansion: Being a Full History of the House on Harlem Heights Built by Roger Morris before the Revolution*, William Henry Shelton writes, "Phebe Bowen's daughters left her, as they grew to young womanhood, to vend their charms in another market, naturally drifting into the life in which they had been reared." They installed themselves in the home of Major Reuben Ballou and his wife, Freelove, described by Shelton as "a sort of doctoress and midwife and otherwise of a shady reputation."

Famed to be the most beautiful girl in Providence, Betsy likely had a thriving small business on her hands. Her time in Providence, though, was brief. Soon after giving birth to a son, George Washington Bowen, on October 9, 1794, Betsy Bowen abandoned her son to the Ballous and left Providence. The woman, who in youth was described as generous of heart and fond of little children, would demonstrate no such kindnesses to her own son.

Betsy Bowen's comely face hid a shrewd mind. After leaving Providence, she took up with a ship's captain named de la Croix. The captain was married, but that didn't stop Betsy from taking his name. She became Madame de la Croix and likely traveled abroad with him. She acquired a cosmopolitan veneer, which played well with rich men. By 1800, Betsy Bowen had traded up and added a name, Brown. No sailor's wench any longer, Betsy Bowen de la Croix Brown had become mistress to one of the wealthiest merchants in New York City, one Stephen Jumel. And this time, Betsy had hit the proverbial jackpot. Monsieur Jumel was a bachelor.

MISTRESS TURNED LADY OF THE MANOR

The two lived in grand fashion. Jumel appeared to adore his beautiful mistress. One of his vessels bore the name the *Eliza*. He installed her in a beautiful house on Whitehall Street in New York. She had a fine carriage at her disposal when such conveyances were fairly rare. And though Betsy Bowen de la Croix Brown likely loved all the pomp and circumstance of her new life, there was one thing that continued to elude her—respectability. New York society was not interested in befriending a whore, no matter how affable or wealthy her lover might be.

Again, Betsy's cleverness was pressed into service. She enlisted the help of a doctor in a ruse to force Jumel into marrying her. The scene was Oscar worthy, befitting what would be the performance of Betsy's life. Jumel returned one day to his Whitehall Street home to find a doctor and a minister attending to Betsy on her deathbed. She would likely not last the night, the unscrupulous quack told Jumel. Betsy, for her part, played the part of the tormented soul, muttering fevered whispers that only the doctor seemed capable of deciphering. He told Jumel that it was his mistress's dying wish to enter heaven a respectable, married woman. Jumel, driven, no doubt, by feelings of love, horror and pity, agreed to a bedside wedding. Madame Jumel made a full recovery twelve hours later.

Jumel's Catholicism compelled him to make the marriage official with a proper church wedding. The pair was married on April 9, 1804, in St. Patrick's Cathedral. It likely wasn't the happy affair Betsy, hereafter Madame Jumel, wanted, however. She had no immediate family in attendance; her parents and sister were dead, and Madame Jumel had made sure to distance herself from her remaining Providence relatives. It is likely that Stephen Jumel knew nothing of her former career as common street whore. The former Betsy Bowen wasn't one to give up secrets easily.

What the pair did in the next eleven years is unclear. They did buy a second home, the Roger Morris House, and set about restoring it to all its colonial glory. The couple also adopted a daughter, Mary Bownes, the child of Betsy's stepsister, Polly Clarke. The adoption of the girl heralded the advent of a disturbing habit of Madame Jumel's. She would, during the course of her life, try to keep young people around her by adopting them, arranging their marriages and then insisting that they live with her. Madame Jumel's controlling nature was no doubt underpinned by serious loneliness. Pity is never enough to bind one to another for too long, though.

And falsehoods' fissures undermine the strongest of foundations. That Madame Jumel's marriage was based on a lie, a promise extracted under false pretenses, must have harmed what true affection Stephen Jumel had for her. Still, he stayed, providing for her every want, even after he learned that she had given birth to and abandoned a child.

Shelton notes that one of the Jumels' servants, Henry Nodine, was called before a court of law to give testimony about the pair's relationship. Though Shelton does not say so, the testimony likely was given in a case concerning the distribution of the Jumel fortune following Madame Jumel's death in 1865. Nodine recounts a furious fight between the pair that ended with Madame Jumel threatening the life of her husband. Nodine's testimony at times sounded as if he were addressing Madame Jumel:

> *You never, never tell Mr. Jumel you had one little boy down in Providence. Else Mr. Jumel would not marry you. That Madam Jumel then admitted the truth: that she cursed and swore at him, and threatened to shoot him with a pistol that she kept and carried.*

This bombshell was followed by the story of how Madame Jumel came to be wife rather than mere mistress. While there is no accounting for how Nodine looked as he delivered the damning story, the tenor of his testimony is clearly one of contempt. Nodine said:

> *You tell Mr. Jumel you very sick and going to die and you want to die one married woman. The doctor tell Mr. Jumel marry you, you die before morning. Mr. Jumel he marry you. In two days you ride around town in your carriage. You tell Mr. Jumel one big story.*

Stephen Jumel must have been one forgiving man, at least initially, because he did not leave his wife after learning of her prior indiscretions. Instead, he, Betsy and their daughter, Mary, boarded the *Eliza* and headed to France.

And that would be the biggest financial mistake of the merchant's illustrious career.

NOBLESSE OBLIGE

The last year of the Jumels' life together was, on one level, a year of triumph for Madame Jumel. She found herself the favorite of the nobility in France. It was, of course, not her winning ways but her open pocketbook that curried favor. She lent noble women her carriage and even allowed a relative of the Empress Josephine to live with her for a time. Stephen Jumel's generosity was in evidence every bit as much as his wife's. One Jumel family legend holds that the pair received a carriage from the Emperor Napoleon himself in gratitude for Stephen's offer of his ship to convey the fallen ruler to America.

Madame Jumel was not allowed to enjoy her newfound status for very long, however. In December 1816, she left France in haste, telling her daughter, Mary, that illness spurred her return to the United States. Stephen Jumel did not return with his wife.

There would be a reconciliation of the Jumel family in 1821, when Madame Jumel returned to Paris. Correspondence between Madame Jumel and French noblewomen indicates that she was able to resurrect the relationships she had cultivated there six years earlier. She worked hard to reestablish herself, once again extending herself and her largess to her social superiors. But she was about to do something that would destroy those carefully cultivated friendships.

Stephen Jumel's fortune was greatly diminished. Some of his ships had been seized and sold by the French government during the Napoleonic Wars, Shelton writes. Jumel did not intend to return to America, but he needed to liquidate his holdings there. He decided to place this task in the eagerly outstretched hand of his wife, giving her power of attorney. For her attention to this matter, Madame Jumel received lifetime use of the couple's New York City property. The last matter settled was that of their separation. Clearly, it was amicable; Stephen would stay in France and Betsy in America with Mary.

Why Jumel trusted his fortune to his wife is a mystery. She had tricked him into marriage and lied about her past. Should it come as any surprise that within a year of her return to America, Madame Jumel began transferring the couple's property titles to her daughter and all revenue generated from them to herself? Betsy Bowen de la Croix Brown Jumel was impervious to her husband's desperate letters and their tales of financial hardship and pleas for money. She wrote to her husband alternately that money was scarce and the property he owned was increasing in value, implying that it shouldn't be sold. When she was done, Madame Jumel had stripped her husband of everything. After years of waiting, Stephen Jumel returned to America in 1828. Betsy headed south, and Jumel was left to feel the full force of his wife's double cross. A broken man, Jumel died four years later and was buried at a Catholic cemetery on Prince Street.

A comfortable living now ensured, Madame Jumel's calculating eye was soon appraising her next target: former vice president of the United States Aaron Burr.

"VICE-QUEEN OF AMERICA"

How well Madame Jumel weathered the news of her husband's passing is unknown. She may have been too busy to give it much thought. Her theft of his estate complete, Madame Jumel turned to the task of finding a proper mate for her adopted daughter, Mary Eliza. This action brought to the fore another dark aspect of Madame Jumel, the part that recalled her days as a former Providence prostitute. The streetwise strumpet in Madame Jumel would ensure that Mary married well. Madame Jumel acted every bit the madam in arranging the marriage between Mary and attorney Nelson Chase. She had met the young man in 1831, arranged the engagement and promised an income to the couple. Her one stipulation: the newlyweds must live with her.

Mary's future secured, Madame Jumel turned to her own. First, she adopted another daughter, Mary Marilla Stever, a seven-year-old child to whom she'd become acquainted when arranging Mary Eliza's marriage. Mary Marilla Stever's parents were willing to part with their daughter, and the girl went to live in the mansion with the fifty-nine-year-old Madame Jumel. Now came perhaps the greatest coup of Madame Jumel's career, for her marriages were, first and foremost, business transactions, and Madame Jumel was a canny businesswoman. On July 3, 1833, Madame Jumel married Aaron Burr, the seventy-eight-year-old former vice president of the United States of America.

Burr's motivation was likely money. He received a groom's gift of $6,000 from his new wife. As for Madame Jumel, there could be only one reason to attach herself to a cash-strapped man twenty-one years her senior: status. Again, she was thwarted. Only two newspapers ran an announcement of the marriage, and both dedicated a mere two lines to the notice. In hindsight, it was probably serendipitous this way. It's likely that few people knew, and fewer still even cared, when the marriage ended less than a year later. This, too, was likely a stroke of luck for Madame Jumel, as she referred to Burr as a "wretch" on at least one occasion.

What Madame Burr liked best about Burr was his name. When she took her last trip to Europe in 1853, the seventy-eight-year-old dowager called herself Madame Burr. In the last years of her life, when senility and insanity had likely set in, Madame Burr told a young visitor to her New York mansion that she was once called the Vice-Queen of America and feared by the French to be a royal assassin. Other fictions told included the claim that the infamous Rhode Island pirate Captain William Kidd buried his treasure on her grounds, that she had had an affair with Alexander Hamilton, that she was in possession of the jewels of Empress Josephine of France and that Dolley Madison and several European kings were her dear friends.

One legend, whether of Madame Jumel's manufacturing or another's is uncertain, is that she was the impetus for the fatal duel between Aaron Burr and Alexander Hamilton. It is highly unlikely that either party had even made her acquaintance in 1804. The old dame's tallest tale was her claim to have refused an offer of marriage from the king of Spain himself. Anyone who knew Madame Jumel must have laughed at this; the calculating social climber would never have turned down the chance to be a queen. It would have been the ultimate trump card for the former Providence strumpet.

MADAME'S DESCENT INTO MADNESS

What was true of the final years of Madame Jumel's life was that she lived a lonely, bitter existence. She had had a terrible fight with the Chases, the family of her first adopted daughter, Mary Eliza, and had thrown them out in 1862.

Shelton characterizes life in the Jumel Mansion as akin to a prison sentence:

> *In arranging* [her nieces'] *marriages, her prime object was to secure more inmates for the mansion, which was dreary for want of fellow beings to speak to. She needed some one* [sic] *to live with, to quarrel with, to drink with... The neighbor families held aloof from her and she knew that their doors were closed to her. The efforts she made to secure companionship in the house were pathetic. She adopted children who left her.*

What Madame Burr's wards learned from her example was to grab whatever they could get. After her death, the fight for Madame Burr's estate was fierce, lasting nearly two decades. The heirs successfully contested her first will, in which she bequeathed a great deal of her fortune to charitable organizations like the Society for the Relief of the Destitute Children of Seamen, the Missionary Society for Seamen in the City and Port of New York and the Association for the Relief of Respectable, Aged, Indigent Females in the City of New York. Clearly, the grand Madame Burr had not forgotten what it was to have been the bastard child of Phebe Kelley.

Most of Madame Burr's fortune was squandered. There were legal fees in the hundreds of thousands of dollars, fed to the lawyers of the various plaintiffs who claimed kinship. There was also theft. An inventory of Madame Burr's estate yielded no diamonds, jewels or sterling silver. Even the spoons and forks had vanished. Still, the heirs squabbled for what remained. Even Burr's bastard son, George Washington Bowen, laid claim to her fortune. George Washington Bowen, along with other Bowens, Vandervoorts, Chases, Joneses and the French branch of the family, the Jumels, filed twenty different cases over sixteen years. Illegitimacy proved too great an obstacle for most, including Madame Jumel's only biological son. Perhaps the court questioned the legitimacy of George Washington Bowen's claim based on others he had made. George Washington Bowen claimed that his father was the father of the country, General George Washington, the first United States president.

He was his mother's son, after all.

It is fair to view Madame Burr as a cold, calculating woman who would spare no one who dared thwart her. Even Madame Burr's beneficent gestures, the generosity she showed her adopted daughters, for example, were ultimately for her benefit. She believed that money could buy her intangibles, like love, friendship and respectability. Her wealth, though, was only in the amassing of a great deal of things. But can a girl who came from so little, who had no education and no prospects, who would have likely died a terrible death after being used by hundreds of indifferent men be blamed for bettering herself the only way she could?

Eliza "Betsy" Bowen de la Croix Brown Jumel Burr was the mistress of many, wife of some and, ultimately, beloved of none. She died insane and paranoid at ninety years of age on July 16, 1865. In a scene so reminiscent of *Great Expectations* as to appear cliché, the former "Vice-Queen of America" lay in state in her "Washington Bedroom," bejeweled and rouged in a cap trimmed with pink ribbons. How like Miss Havisham she must have appeared. And, like Miss Havisham, she suffered the greatest of indignities: to die unmourned, forgotten and alone.

⌑

DOLLY COLE:
THE TRANSVESTITE PROSTITUTE/VAMPIRE/ WITCH OF FOSTER?

It is no easy thing to write about Dolly Cole. First, the legend that is Dolly Cole is likely the story of two women: Dorothy Ellen Cole and Dolly Cole, both of whom lived and died in Foster. A brook, a bridge and a pond in the town bear the name Dolly Cole, conferring upon the two a degree of respectability that neither enjoyed in life.

Rumor has it that there is one extant historical record of the death of a Dorothy Cole of Foster. On its website, the Rhode Island Paranormal Research Group and Society (RIPRGS) asserts that a local newspaper reported on her likely murder. Dorothy Cole's body was found in the vicinity of Foster's Ramtail Road, and the 1893 newspaper account suggests foul play. RIPRGS posits that the girl's death was overshadowed by the highly publicized 1893 trial and acquittal of Fall River, Massachusetts's Lizzie Borden. Borden was accused of murdering her father and stepmother with an axe in their Fall River home. Was Dorothy Cole's murder investigation ignored by local reporters in favor of the more salacious Borden tragedy? Perhaps. Certainly, if Dorothy Cole was a cross-dressing prostitute, as some allege, then townsfolk may have dismissed her murder as not worthy of note.

Depending on who is telling the story, Dolly Cole is a lovely, young, brunette woman in white who haunts the shooting range of a private gun club in the area. Or she's wearing men's clothing as she bends over a pond to fill a pail with water. Some would say she's a vampire; others, a witch. Still others maintain that Dolly Cole was a transvestite prostitute who ran into the wrong john. And then there's the tale of her having cursed the whole town after its residents burned her house and her family with it. It is almost impossible to separate fact from fiction where Dolly Cole is concerned. A better approach, perhaps, is to examine three legends independently.

LEGEND I. DOLLY COLE: CURSE OF THE WITCH

In this version, Dolly Cole is suspected by her neighbors of being a witch. Foster, by the way, is the leading contender for the Rhode Island town claiming the most witches—seventeen. According to legend, the townsfolk decided to do away with the entire Cole family. Unlike their Salem, Massachusetts neighbors, Foster's vigilantes did not wait for a trial to exact justice. They waited for the cover of darkness to do their dark deed, setting the Cole house on fire as its inhabitants slept. The house became the Cole family's funeral pyre, a hellish blaze that engulfed the home, leaving only its foundation remaining. But was Dolly in the home at the time?

Here again, accounts vary. In one, the young Dolly had left the house to fetch a pail of water before the attack commenced. When she returned to find her home ablaze and her young daughter surely dead, Dolly cursed the town, promising that its inhabitants would be visited by terrible disease and death. In another version of the tale, Dolly was able to escape the blaze, crawling from it on all fours, felled by heat and smoke. Her final moments were likely ones of searing pain: cooked from the outside in, Dolly collapsed and died in a swamp on her property.

What evidence did the townspeople have of Dolly Cole's wicked ways? She had helped her neighbors with their illnesses, providing them with herbal remedies to ease their suffering. She may also have had the gift of sight, the ability to see into the future. Of course, nowadays, many would chalk such talent up to intuition.

At any rate, it is the same old story. A woman uses her gifts for the good of the community and is victimized. The postscript to this version of the legend is that many hunters say they have seen a dark-haired woman in outdated men's clothing walking through the swamp. They always mistake the ghost for a living woman; that is, until she disappears. No theory as to why her ghost haunts the area has been advanced. Perhaps she is looking for the members of her long-dead family.

LEGEND II. DOLLY COLE: CROSS-DRESSING PROSTITUTE

This second tale of Dorothy "Dolly" Cole holds that she did not die in a fire but likely suffered the fate of many in her line of work—that of murder victim. This version of the legend incorporates the murder that was recounted in the local newspaper but embellishes it, claiming that she was a transvestite prostitute. Also, this version says that her dead body was dumped in the roadside brook that bears her name rather than at the Ramtail Road address given in the newspaper account. *Haunted Rhode Island* author Thomas D'Agostino recounts in his book that it was at the Dolly Cole Brook where he, as a boy of eleven, witnessed the figure of a young woman approaching him. Surprised that he had not heard her approach, D'Agostino looked away from her, gazing about for his father. When he turned back, the girl was gone.

LEGEND III. DOLLY COLE: VAMPIRE

Folklorists often note that in the telling and retelling of a story, facts fall away and fiction is added. It feels wrong not to mention that it has been said that Dolly Cole was a vampire. Certainly, Rhode Island has a rich folkloric tradition where vampires are concerned. At this writing, however, accounts of Dolly Cole, vampire, have yet to be discovered. It is not too much of a stretch to think that the people of Foster, in creating their own personal ogre, would gift her with multiple malevolent capabilities. And doesn't it stand to reason that the more evil the scapegoat seems, the more vindicated her tormentors feel for their part in her demise?

Fellow Rhode Islander and Pulitzer Prize–winner Edith Wharton wrote in her famous ghost story "Afterward" of a spirit whose haunting of human beings would go unnoticed and unremarked upon in the moment of its happening. Those poor souls to experience the ghost and its ghastly mission would only know they'd been haunted long afterward. So it goes with Dolly Cole, according to those who have seen her. The accounts agree on a single point: to look away from the lovely woman of the wood is to lose her, and all that is left is wonder long afterward. Who is that specter in the wood and why does she continue to haunt the town of Foster? And why are people still so fascinated by her?

In this respect, Dolly Cole has cast a spell.

HULDY CRADDOCK:
HOUSEKEEPER FROM HELL

Legend has it that Huldy Craddock was the housekeeper to one Captain Japeth Wedderburn, a wealthy sea captain who made his home in Narragansett in its fashionable Pier neighborhood. The Wedderburn Mansion was likely similar to those sprawling, weathered structures with a view of Narragansett Bay.

It was rumored that Huldy was in love with her employer, so she probably didn't take it well when Wedderburn arrived home from an overseas voyage with a beautiful, young Spanish wife. Donna Mercedes Wedderburn was a petite beauty given to wearing the fashions of her native country, which included a black lace mantilla, a scarf that covered her head and shoulders held in place by a tortoise shell comb.

It was not, however, Donna Mercedes's exotic clothing that drew others' attention. Neighbors who caught a glimpse of the girl spoke of the sorrow and longing that she wore on her face when she gazed out the windows of her home. Wedderburn rarely took his wife out in society, and some whispered that the girl was the prisoner of a jealous, volatile husband.

Then one day, the lovely Donna Mercedes disappeared. Wedderburn told those who inquired that he had returned Mercedes to her homeland. The captain remained single for the rest of his days, his only company the loyal Huldy Craddock. Dark rumors ran rampant in the quiet, seaside community, telling of a jealous husband who would never have voluntarily let his young wife go and a housekeeper willing to do what was necessary to keep her employer from jail. Some stories held that Wedderburn murdered his wife when she begged for release. Others said that Huldy dealt the deathblow in her own fit of jealous rage.

And though there was no doubt that the girl was gone, visitors to the Wedderburn Mansion occasionally noted the specter of a young, foreign girl wearing a Spanish mantilla walking the rooms of the mansion and sobbing.

It was some years later when the fate of Donna Mercedes would come to light. Subsequent owners of the Wedderburn Mansion were renovating a fireplace when they made a horrific discovery. Entombed behind the stone, in a manner befitting an Edgar Allan Poe tale, a skeleton was found wearing, among other things, a tattered mantilla and a tortoise shell comb.

What Huldy Craddock's role was in the demise of Donna Mercedes is unknown. In fact, nothing exists but the legend of Craddock's and Wedderburn's misdeeds. There is no evidence that there ever was a Wedderburn Mansion in Narragansett, for that matter. All that remains is a sordid tale of an alleged misdeed veiled in mystery and a shrouded ghost eternally pining for her homeland.

⋇

FORBIDDEN FRUIT SOLD LOCALLY

Adam's Eve is the original fallen woman and, to many, a witch as well. What she might not be is repentant. In fact, Eve might have sought to share her hard-won wealth at one time. One Rhode Island story holds that a sixteenth-century gentleman farmer once received a nocturnal visit from Eden's legendary outcast, who had gardening tips on how to successfully grow forbidden fruit from the Tree of Knowledge in Portsmouth soil.

The legend, according to John T. Pierce Sr.'s 1991 *Historical Tracts of the Town of Portsmouth, Rhode Island*, goes like this: There was a wealthy privateer by the name of Metcalf Bowler who had a summer residence on Portsmouth's Wapping Road. Bowler was a world traveler who made his fortune in the Triangular Trade. The merchant's vessels would set sail from the colonies headed for the West Indies with a cargo of lumber, salted fish and grain. There he traded his stores for molasses, which he then took to various New England ports, where the sticky stuff was turned into rum. This, in turn, was taken to Africa and traded for human cargo—slaves.

When not engaged in his nefarious business dealings, Bowler indulged his passion for gardening. On his Portsmouth home's property was a magnificent garden, replete with hothouses for his more exotic acquisitions. His most prized possession was not the expected Egyptian white water lily or a sacred Indian lotus, however. It wasn't a Brazilian dancing lady orchid or a bird of paradise, either, though Paradise was the priceless plant's origin.

The Fall of Man by Hendrik Goltzius, 1616.

One of Bowler's ship captains, a man by the name of Green Chausan, rescued a Persian prince from certain death by shipwreck. When Captain Chausan returned the prince to his homeland of Assyria, the young man's father, a king, presented Chausan with a seedling, an apple tree said to be from the Garden of Eden itself. Moreover, the Persian king claimed the apple tree to be descended from the Tree of Knowledge. When Captain Chausan returned to Rhode Island, he made a gift of the tree to Bowler. Bowler was thrilled, of course, to receive such a matchless gift and thought to put it in one of his greenhouses to ensure its safety.

Enter Eve.

Her apparition came to Bowler in a dream and admonished him to refrain from locking the tree away in a hothouse. If anything, Eve said, Portsmouth's soil was better than Eden's for cultivating this apple. Not one to question the advice of the supernatural, Bowler planted his cultivar in Portsmouth soil and named it the Rhode Island Greening.

And so the fruit of the Tree of Knowledge can be found at your local Rhode Island orchard from October through mid-November. Eat at your own risk.

Hell's Half Acre

The venerable American Patriot Benjamin Franklin once said, "Certainty? In this world nothing is certain but death and taxes." He might well have added prostitution to the adage.

Historically, women of no means, talent or education have had few options available to them when it came to supporting themselves. The lucky ones found mates; the unlucky, madams.

Before the advent of welfare programs and housing for the destitute, Rhode Island women in trouble had little choice but to turn to the world's oldest profession, prostitution, to eke out a living. Contrary to what colonial- and Victorian-era societies believed, a girl did not choose prostitution because of her essentially seductive nature. Prostitution, simply, was much more likely a pragmatic decision spurred by necessity. A woman had to eat and, oftentimes, feed her family as well. And even in the direst economic times, there was always a market for a prostitute's services.

If a nineteenth-century man were looking for companionship in the southern part of the state, he was ensured success if he went to Hell's Half Acre, an area in West Greenwich demarcated by Widow Sweet's and Congdon Mill Roads. Here, working girls would congregate in the many inns and taverns that dotted the roads, tempting weary travelers with food, drink, gambling and, of course, companionship for the night.

According to Kelly Sullivan Pezza's 2006 book, *History, Mystery and Lore of Rhode Island,* when business slowed, the wenches of Hell's Half Acre made house calls. A carriage would be hired to ferry the girls to the various mills in the area to add a little spice to the millworker's lunch.

Pezza says that Hell's Half Acre received its name from a minister. He was likely an abolitionist. Victorian-era abolitionists thought to stop prostitution by offering shelter, at least temporarily, in return for a fallen woman's repentance. What the abolitionists couldn't or didn't offer was alternative employment. The minister was said to have visited various establishments, trying to convince the women to reject their wicked ways. When the man of God failed in his mission, he gave the women up for lost, naming the area where they plied their wares Hell's Half Acre.

⁘

THE MAD MAMA OF BLOCK ISLAND

Legend has it that Block Island played host to a malevolent lot of marauders called wreckers. Like the sirens of Greek legend, the wreckers of Block Island would lure ships to its sandy shores with the intention of looting them and bludgeoning their passengers. Horrid enough on its own, this island welcome was not reserved just for strangers. An islander who left his home might find the price of return perilous.

No date or last name survives in the story of Bill, an island boy who ran away from home to find adventure at sea. Sometime later, Bill returned to the island on a vessel lured there by the wreckers. Ethel Colt Ritchie recounted the details of the story, given to her by an islander, in her 1955 book, *Block Island Lore and Legends*. Ritchie relates his story as follows:

> One dark and stormy night the buzzards tied a lantern to a horse's tail and run it round and round a haystack to make it look like it was hung in a ship rigging riding in a rough sea. Any ship that saw that light would steer a like course and end up on the shore. One did. And on it was a Block Island lad who had run away to sea, but was on his way back to see his mother. The "wrackers" were out and his mother with them.

That night, the choppy seas and violent winds conspired with the wreckers, and their lure proved fatal for the ship's crew. Only one sailor survived. The sea spared young Bill, and he, no doubt, thought the harrowing portion of his trial to be behind him as he dragged himself out of the breakwater.

His mother met him there and, the old islander told Ritchie, "he was sure glad to see his mother until she leaned over him and said, 'Bill, you know the island rules.' And with that she up and hit him over the head with a 'pebble' and shoved him back into the undertow."

The story ends there, with a madwoman braining her prodigal son on the shores of their beloved home. Whatever other "rules" the wreckers lived by, this was surely the most severe.

CATHERINE MOUNT: GUILTY BY ASSOCIATION

Colonial courts didn't discriminate between criminals and their mates. Any woman who would cavort with a criminal was held in contempt by colonial society. If one were the bride of a criminal, the vow for better or worse could entail jail time.

If Catherine Mount had a hand in the crimes of her husband, Thomas, colonial court records make no mention of it. What is recorded, however, is Catherine's incarceration in Rhode Island jails in Newport and Little Rest, now Kingston. Catherine was kept in the Washington County Jail while her husband awaited death by hanging, a sentence executed on May 27, 1791. Thomas was the last man to be executed in Washington County.

Catherine had the misfortune of falling in love with a career criminal. At the time of his execution, twenty-seven-year-old Thomas had admitted to ninety-five counts of thievery, capping a career that began in his youth with crimes of stealing apples from orchards and behaving disrespectfully toward his parents, writes Christopher P. Bickford in his 2002 book, *Crime, Punishment and the Washington County Jail: Hard Time in Kingston, Rhode Island*. Too bad Thomas couldn't steal a little contrition along the way. Bickford writes that for bad behavior in the courtroom during one of his trials, Thomas received 125 lashes.

What must Catherine have thought to see her husband dragged from the jail at Little Rest and sent to the gallows for the theft of two shillings and six pence worth of cotton cloth he'd taken from a store in Hopkinton. Did Catherine remain in her cell during Thomas's final moments, or was she permitted to be with her husband at the hour of his death? She wasn't executed, that much is certain.

In life, Thomas had the reputation for being as adept at breaking out of buildings as breaking into them. He had escaped jails in Boston, Philadelphia and Fairfield, Connecticut. A dozen men stood guard at the Little Rest jail to ensure that Thomas kept his appointment on May 27. What became of Catherine after that day is unknown.

Perhaps Thomas wasn't the only escape artist in the family.

⬥⬥⬥

EVELYN NESBIT:
VIXEN OR VICTIM?

If Helen of Troy had an American counterpart, it was Evelyn Nesbit. The embodiment of feminine beauty, Nesbit prefigured the pinup girl and the supermodel. She was, some contend, the Marilyn Monroe of her age.

What she was not was a Rhode Islander. At least, not in life. Yet Nesbit's story is intertwined in the art and architecture of Newport so completely that the city has become, in a way, the custodian of her memory.

Nesbit was the one-time mistress of Stanford White, the internationally known architect of the Newport Casino, Rosecliff Mansion and the Isaac Bell House. White had a yearlong affair with Nesbit and was murdered by her jealous husband, Harry Kendall Thaw, in 1906. White was shot, pointblank, three times in the face at a theatre performance in Madison Square Garden, also a building of his design.

The affair was over at the time of White's murder. Thaw, though, was obsessed with White. He may have had reason. Evelyn Nesbit was not over White when she married Thaw. White, however, was done with her. Perhaps Nesbit missed the excitement of the affair. After all, White had once enlisted a Newport socialite's and a New York theatre troupe's assistance in a scheme for a single night in Newport with Nesbit—a heady thrill for a young chorus girl.

THE WOLF AND THE WAIF

When talking of Stanford White, architects and art historians inevitably link the famed designer to the City by the Sea. Stanford White certainly left his imprimatur on Newport. The third member of the famed architectural triumvirate McKim, Mead and White, White initially made his mark in American architecture designing Shingle-style summer cottages for the fabulously wealthy. Among the firm's finest achievements is the Newport Casino, housing the International Tennis Hall of Fame, where the Stanford White Casino Theatre is located.

White's eye for beauty extended beyond the realm of architecture. White was known for his philandering and his taste for young women—

girls, by modern standards. White spotted sixteen-year-old chorus girl Nesbit in the production *Florodora* and, initially, played the role of patron. Nesbit was supporting her mother, brother and herself with her modeling and acting work. White, appealing to both the girl and the woman, plied Nesbit with gifts of toys, jewels, furs and meals. On one occasion, White presented her with a red cloak, a gift that would characterize their sordid relationship. In effect, Evelyn played Little Red Riding Hood to White's Big, Bad Wolf. At some point, the relationship turned sexual. He was forty-seven, she was sixteen.

After White's murder, Henry Thaw's mother spent a great deal of the family fortune on her son's defense and, legend says, promised her daughter-in-law $1 million if she would testify to the nature of her relationship with White. Nesbit did, revealing what must have been deeply embarrassing details of the affair. One anecdote in particular, involving the sixteen-year-old virginal Nesbit riding on a red velvet swing while White watched, was undoubtedly mortifying in the retelling. Nesbit wrote two memoirs, both of which include the story. She writes in *The Story of My Life*:

> We went up another two flights of stairs, and came to the room at the top of the building. My first impression of the room was that extended in the very centre was a large velvet chair swinging on two ropes from the ceiling, and above this chair, closer to the ceiling, was hung a big open Japanese umbrella of paper.
>
> "Let me give you a swing," said Stanford White. I got into the chair and he swung me higher and higher, till I almost touched the umbrella.
>
> "I want to see your feet go through it," he said, swinging me more vigorously; and soon after I accomplished what he desired, for my feet went crashing through the paper cover of the umbrella. It was amusing. I enjoyed it thoroughly. I did not realize that childish fun could have any serious significance. I did not realize that this prepossessing and kindly man could have any other object in view than to amuse me.

In August 1902, actress Nesbit would visit Newport with the entire cast of *The Wild Rose* for an unprecedented event. The cast and an orchestra performed the play for Mrs. Cornelius Vanderbilt at Beaulieu, her Newport cottage designed by Stanford White, of course. Nesbit's biographer, Paula Uruburu, in her book, *American Eve: Evelyn Nesbit, Stanford White, the Birth of the "It" Girl and the Crime of the Century*, would characterize the event as the "One-Night Stand in Newport."

Nesbit would testify at Thaw's murder trial that her husband's motivation was more than jealous rage; it was the defense of her honor after hearing her tell of such stories. But neither her testimony nor his mother's money would spare Thaw. He was found to be insane, convicted of murder and incarcerated in an asylum.

As for Nesbit, she had a son, Russell, whom she insisted was Thaw's, but the timing of the pregnancy and birth were suspect. When released from prison, Thaw denied that he was the boy's father, saying that he had been incarcerated at the time of conception. Nesbit returned to the stage and married again, but neither career nor marriage brought her happiness. She became an alcoholic and attempted suicide more than once. Nesbit died in a nursing home in 1967 at the age of eighty-two.

AMERICAN IDOL

Like Marilyn Monroe, Nesbit enjoys a peculiar celebrity in death. Her testimony about White's seduction swing inspired the 1955 movie *The Girl in the Red Velvet Swing* and, twenty-five years later, E.L. Doctorow's novel *Ragtime*. And *Anne of Green Gables* fans may be surprised to find that the title character of author Lucy Maude Montgomery's series owes her inspiration to Evelyn Nesbit.

Similarly inspired was Stanford White's friend, American illustrator Charles Dana Gibson. Nesbit played muse to Gibson, who used her visage to create his iconic, signature image—the Gibson Girl. Much of his work now resides in Newport's National Museum of American Illustration at Vernon Court.

Art historians contend that Gibson's wife, Irene Langhorne Gibson, was the true prototype for the Gibson Girl. The comparison of the illustration to Nesbit, though, would certainly explain how the legend arose. If not Gibson's inspiration, Nesbit was equally worthy of the artist's notice. Nesbit, too, possessed the angel's face and the harlot's figure; she was innocence and sexuality embodied in one. It is a widely held belief that Gibson's famous illustration *Eternal Question* is of Nesbit.

In 2009, a portrait of Nesbit turned up in the Newport Art Museum show entitled "Focus on Four," prompting a *Providence Journal* reporter to characterize Nesbit as "a famous Gilded Age beauty who manages to exude more sex appeal while fully (albeit suggestively) clothed than a year's worth

The angelic face of Evelyn Nesbit Thaw, one of American illustrator Charles Dana Gibson's legendary Gibson Girls, graced many a postcard. *Author's collection.*

"Gibson's Typical American Girl" was anything but. *Author's collection.*

of Playboy centerfolds." In the same year, the Stanford White/Evelyn Nesbit affair was included in another *Providence Journal* article entitled "Who Killed the American Renaissance?" The reporter does not argue definitively that White's murder heralded the demise of the American Renaissance movement, but he does suggest that it is a plausible possibility. He also includes portraits of White, Nesbit and Thaw. He's likely right. How much power can one beautiful woman wield, after all? It's as absurd to think a woman could spur a lover to murder a rival and, by association, an artistic movement as it is to believe a woman might inspire ancient armies to wage years of war.

What is certain, though, is that, even today, Rhode Island covets the cursed Nesbit as much as any admirer could. Wanton or wretch, she remains ever its mistress.

❈

Mary Rosse and Her Womanly Wiles

Colonial courts were pretty indiscriminate in their punishments, the stocks and whipping posts being adequate for most crimes. Modern courts, however, strive to mete punishments equal in severity to the egregiousness of the offense. Contemporary lawmakers recognize that stealing a pack of gum isn't the same thing as holding up the entire store. Theft of a bicycle doesn't carry the same punishment as grand theft auto.

But then there are crimes that are just mean. Like when you mess with a man's dog, his house and his kids. Such were the crimes of Mary Rosse. If ever a woman deserved the term "wench," it would be Rosse.

In 1683, Mary Rosse and Jonathan Dunham broke into the Little Compton home of John Irish. The two were vagrants; Dunham had faced Massachusetts courts for his vagrancy and "corrupt principles," writes Diane Rapaport in *The Naked Quaker: True Crimes and Controversies from the Courts of Colonial New England*. He likely was charged with the latter for carrying on with Rosse, as he was already a husband and a father.

According to court records, Rosse and Dunham entered the Irish home and killed the man's dog. Then, they started a fire and threw the poor dog's body on it. What followed next was pure insanity, if one assumes that the criminals intended to survive their crime. Rosse and Dunham barred Irish from entering the home, the home that they had just set on fire. This colonial-era Bonnie and Clyde had barricaded themselves, along with the Irish children, in a burning house. Irish managed to rescue the children with the help of neighbors.

In the court case that followed, neither Rosse nor Dunham denied the charges leveled against them. Dunham, however, chose to mount a classic argument: Adam's Eve-made-me-do-it defense. He said he was under a spell, captivated by Rosse's "enthusiastical power," according to Rapaport. It was as good a defense as any. The belief in women as seductive, immoral beings was certainly not a new idea to colonial New Englanders. And, to some degree, the evil temptress defense tactic worked. Dunham was whipped and banished. Rosse, though, was whipped multiple times and escorted out of Plymouth County by several constables.

Rosse's power over Dunham must have been formidable, indeed. Six years later, the pair turned up in New Jersey. Dunham bought land and a house there, deeded it over to Rosse and then returned to his wife and family. Rosse took up with another married man, who had left his pregnant wife for her. When the abandoned wife brought suit against the pair, Rosse returned the deed of the house to Dunham and fled for New York with her new partner.

What became of Mary Rosse is unknown, which is unusual considering she seemed to make an impression wherever she went.

PART III
WILD WOMEN

ALVA VANDERBILT BELMONT:
AMERICAN TIGRESS

Alva Erskine Vanderbilt Belmont was no ordinary Newport socialite. In her public and private life, she was a formidable force, earning her the nickname "Bengal tiger."

Like her feline counterpart, Alva was a predator. Her prey changed over time. Early in her adult life, Alva sought dominance over New York society. Later, her quarry became an aristocratic title for her daughter, Consuelo. In her advanced years, Alva sought women's suffrage, donating $1 million to that effort. A staunch feminist before such a term existed, the indomitable Alva is rumored to have said, "Just pray to God. She will help you."

Born in Mobile, Alabama, in 1853, Alva was twenty-two when she married into one of America's wealthiest families: the Vanderbilts. William Kissam Vanderbilt was the grandson of Commodore Cornelius Vanderbilt, the railroad magnate. Together they had three children: Consuelo, William K. Jr. and Harold.

The Vanderbilts' was not a happy marriage, wrote Consuelo in her autobiography, *The Glitter and the Gold*:

Alva Vanderbilt Belmont, socialite turned suffragette.

Alva Vanderbilt's Marble House.

Why my parents ever married remains a mystery to me. They were both delightful, charming and intelligent people, but wholly unsuited to each other. My father, although deep in his business interests, found life a happy adventure. His gentle nature hated strife. I still feel pain at the thought of the unkind messages I was made the bearer of when, in the months that preceded their parting, my mother no longer spoke to him. The purport of those messages I no longer remember—they were, I believe, concerned with the divorce she desired and with her wishes and decrees regarding custody of the children and arrangements for the future. My father had a generous and unselfish nature; his pleasure was to see people happy and he enjoyed the company of his children and friends, but my mother—for reasons I can but ascribe to a towering ambition—opposed these carefree views with all the force of her strong personality. Her combative nature rejoiced in conquests. She loved a fight. A born dictator, she dominated events about her as thoroughly as she eventually dominated her husband and her children. If she admitted another point of view she never conceded; we were pawns in her game to be moved as her wishes decreed.

Alva first focused her "towering ambition" on besting the queen of New York society, Caroline Schermerhorn Astor, or Mrs. Astor, as she was better known. Mrs. Astor was the architect of New York society in her creation of the Four Hundred, a social circle of four hundred persons from old money families fit to be in Mrs. Astor's company. Alva, a new money socialite, was not initially Astor A-list material. Alva returned insult with snub, inviting twelve hundred of New York's finest to a costume ball, a grand housewarming event to celebrate the completion of Alva's New York mansion. Alva's invite list was three times that of Mrs. Astor's, but there was no room to be spared for society's grand dame. Mrs. Astor, perhaps motivated by the dismay of her daughter at not receiving an invitation, paid Alva a visit, a sign in their rarified world of being accepted into society. In this way, an invitation was extended, and Alva's social status was cemented.

This coup demonstrated that Alva's towering ambition was underpinned by iron determination. What she couldn't gain with money, Alva acquired with moxie. And nothing, not even her daughter's happiness, would halt her.

MARRIAGE BROKER

Consuelo viewed herself as part of her mother's staging. She was a possession—a prized possession, but a possession, nonetheless. Consuelo's reminiscences of the Vanderbilts' Newport home, Marble House, attest to her feelings that she was Alva's property. Of her bedroom in the Marble House, Consuelo writes:

> *An unadorned stone mantel opposite my bed greeted my waking eyes. To the right on an antique table were aligned a mirror and various silver brushes and combs. On another table writing utensils were disposed in such perfect order that I never ventured to use them. For my mother had chosen every piece of furniture and had placed every ornament according to her taste, and had forbidden the intrusion of my personal possessions. Often as I lay on the bed, that like St. Ursula's in the lovely painting by Carpaccio stood on a dais and was covered with a badaquin, I reflected that there was in her love of me something of the creative spirit of an artist—that it was her wish to produce me as a finished specimen framed in a perfect setting, and that my person was dedicated to whatever final disposal she had in mind.*

Consuelo, though, soon learned that she would not be her mother's window dressing forever. Alva wanted a title for her daughter and, in 1863, found one—for a price. The Duke of Marlborough needed big money to keep himself in the manner to which he'd grown accustomed, and Alva was happy to oblige.

The wedding was arranged, despite the resistance of Consuelo, who was in love with another. Alva, upon learning of the other man, whom Consuelo refers to as Mr. X, showed her steely will once more. She spirited her daughter away from her lover and intercepted all letters between the two. Like Consuelo, the Duke of Marlborough loved another, but, unlike his soon-to-be bride, Marlborough willingly forsook love for money. Perhaps it was the recollection of this unhappy arrangement that led Alva to later say, "First marry for money. Then marry for love."

Though Consuelo was an accommodating creature, at the news of her engagement, she rebelled. The battle was protracted and legendary. Consuelo writes:

> *On reaching Newport my life became that of a prisoner, with my mother and my governess as wardens. I was never out of their sight. Friends called but were told I was not at home. Locked behind those high walls—the porter had orders not to let me out unaccompanied—I had no chance of getting any word to my fiancé. Brought up to obey, I was helpless under my mother's total domination.*

Consuelo told her mother that she intended to marry Mr. X. Alva the tigress went for the jugular. Consuelo writes:

> *I suffered every searing reproach, heard every possible invective hurled at the man I loved. I was informed of his numerous flirtations, of his well-known love for a married woman, of his desire to marry an heiress. My mother even declared that he would have no children and that there was madness in his family...In a final appeal to my feelings she argued that her decision to select a husband for me was founded on considerations I was too young and inexperienced to appreciate. Though rent by so emotional a plea, I still maintained my right to lead the life I wished. It was perhaps my unexpected resistance or the mere fact that no one had ever stood up to her that made her say she would not hesitate to shoot a man whom she considered would ruin my life.*

The day after this fight, a Mrs. Jay, a friend of Alva's who was staying at Marble House with the family, informed Consuelo that their argument the night before had resulted in Alva having a heart attack. Consuelo asked the woman if her mother would reconsider. Mrs. Jay reiterated Alva's claim that she was resolved to commit murder rather than see her daughter marry Mr. X. Moreover, Mrs. Jay said, further conflict would likely result in Alva's death. Consuelo relented. Alva rallied, making a remarkably quick recovery.

On November 6, 1894, a distraught Consuelo became the Duchess of Marlborough. Of her wedding day, she writes:

> *I felt cold and numb as I went down to meet my father and the bridesmaids who were waiting for me. My mother had decreed that my father should accompany me to the church to give me away. After that he was to disappear. We were twenty minutes late, for my eyes, swollen with the tears I had wept, required copious sponging before I could face the curious stares that always greet a bride.*

Consuelo would suffer through an unhappy marriage for eleven years before obtaining a divorce. Alva later said that forcing Consuelo into a loveless marriage was one of her greatest regrets.

SOCIALITE TURNED SUFFRAGETTE

Alva married a second time, choosing as her husband her first husband's best friend, Oliver H.P. Belmont. The pair's union was short, twelve years. After Belmont's death, Alva would undertake her greatest challenge: women's rights. One source said that Alva spent $1 million on the cause and founded the Political Equality Association. It was during this period of Alva's life that she was dubbed Alabama's Bengal tiger by writer John Sledge. In 1914, Alva joined what was to become the National Women's Party. Alva died in 1933. Her casket was borne from the church by an exclusively female contingent of pallbearers. One of the former socialite's last directives was that pictures of her in her youth be destroyed. It appears that Alva the suffragette had little tolerance for Alva the socialite.

What vestigial friction existed between Alva and Consuelo appeared to end before Alva's death. Like her mother, in her post-divorce years Consuelo had devoted herself to women's causes. Perhaps their mutual interests overrode their tempestuous past. What is clear is that Consuelo admired her mother, and if one who suffered so keenly could forgive, then how can anyone else cast aspersions? Perhaps, like the Bengal tiger's, Alva's actions were completely in keeping with her nature.

⊰⊱

MARY DYER: AMERICAN MARTYR

Mary Dyer was marked for death before she was even born. The highest authorities in two countries would pursue her with the intention of killing her. The second would succeed.

Dyer was likely the daughter of English royalty. Legend has it that she was the only child born to Arabella Stuart and Sir William Seymour, who were secretly married in 1610. The reason for the secrecy was that King James I had forbidden his first cousin Arabella from marrying for fear that a successful suitor would also succeed in wresting the throne from him. Arabella's marriage to Seymour, a descendant of King Henry II, and her subsequent pregnancy further fueled James's fears. The two royals had produced an heir, and an heir was a threat.

King James had Arabella sent to Highgate Prison and Seymour to the Tower of London. Arabella tried to escape but was apprehended and sent to the tower. She spent the last four years of her life imprisoned. Seymour successfully escaped the tower and fled to France, where he stayed until James's death. He returned to England to tutor the future King Charles II.

What of the infant? The baby, a girl, was left in the care of Mary Dyer, a lady-in-waiting to Arabella. Dyer hid the child's parentage by giving the baby her name. She also left court to raise the child in the country. Like Jesus Christ and Moses before him, Mary, too, was hunted by a jealous king. James I sent men in search of the child and, like his predecessors, was thwarted.

At twenty-two, Mary married William Dyer, and the two arrived in America in 1635. There they joined the Puritan community that had established the Massachusetts Bay Colony and the Boston Congregational Church. Plain, simple and strict are apt adjectives to describe the Puritan

85

Mary Dyer's memorial marker at Founders' Brook Park, Portsmouth. *Photo by M.E. Reilly-McGreen.*

lifestyle. The church scrutinized every aspect of a person's life. One edict held that women were not allowed to speak on the sermons they heard in church. Mary, though, soon found herself questioning such ideas when she joined friend Anne Hutchinson in a weekly discussion group that did just that. When Anne ventured further to say that God spoke directly to his people through their consciences—a heresy—Mary readily supported her.

Freethinking proved a dangerous indulgence for Mary Dyer. In 1638, she and her husband were banished from the colony. They moved to Portsmouth, Rhode Island, and there, together with the Hutchinsons and others, established the Portsmouth (Rhode Island) Compact. This action was historic for the philosophy inherent in its creation. Composed by colonist John Clarke, the compact's goal was the establishment of a society whose members could worship as they pleased. Scholars have cited this philosophy as the reason why no women were charged, convicted or executed for the crime of witchcraft in the state of Rhode Island.

The timing of the compact could not have been better for Mary. In 1637, she delivered a stillborn infant girl with visible deformities. Anne Hutchinson,

Mary's midwife, secretly buried the infant, as she knew that news of the stillbirth could put Dyer's life in jeopardy. The birth of a deformed infant to a woman who had criticized Puritan law would be interpreted as just punishment sent by God. A year later, Massachusetts Bay Colony governor John Winthrop, a political enemy of Dyer and Hutchinson, gave credence to Hutchinson's fears. When Winthrop learned of the stillborn child, he used news of this unfortunate birth to advance his idea that women like Dyer were handmaidens of the devil. That another woman at the birth, Goody Hawkins, testified that the child had horns, clawed feet and no face only bolstered his case.

Mary Dyer had other children, and by 1650, she and William had built a home in Newport. What prompted her at that point to leave her husband and six children behind while she sailed to England is unknown, says her biographer Ruth Plimpton in *Mary Dyer: Biography of a Rebel Quaker*. What is known is that while Mary was there, she converted to a new religion: Quakerism. Its appeal for Mary was likely that Quakers, like Mary, believed in a personal relationship with God. Quakers were also notorious non-joiners; they didn't believe in war, making oaths or tipping their hats to persons of status in the community.

When Mary returned to the colonies, she visited those Quakers who had been imprisoned in Boston. Punishments for Quakers were fierce in colonial America. Men and women were often publicly scourged; stripped naked to the waist, they were tied to the backs of horse and cattle carts and whipped as they were pulled down the street. Cutting off the ear of an avowed Quaker was another punishment, and the second ear followed if necessary. The branding of a "B" for blasphemy was still another punitive measure. Finally, if a colonist persisted in her alternative religion, death by hanging proved her final deterrent.

Mary Dyer visited Boston on four different occasions in the final years of her life. The first and second times she was imprisoned. On the third, she was sentenced to death and only learned of her reprieve after the noose had been placed around her neck.

The fourth time proved fatal for Mary. On June 1, 1660, Mary Dyer marched once more from prison to the gallows at Boston Commons. Then governor John Endicott ordered drumming to drown out the protests of supporters. Still, some could be heard yelling, "Go back to Rhode Island where you might save your life!" and "Go back and live!" writes Plimpton. Dyer did not live. There was no eleventh-hour reprieve this time.

Like her friend Anne Hutchison, Mary Dyer has a statue in her likeness in Massachusetts's capital city. It is accompanied by a quotation, which reads, "My Life not Availeth Me in Comparison to The Liberty of the Truth." Like his predecessor Governor Winthrop, John Endicott had succeeded in ridding the colonies of another rebellious woman. But it was a short-lived victory. Upon hearing news of Mary Dyer's death, King Charles II wrote to Endicott that Quakers should not be executed but sent back to England.

The message was hand delivered to the governor by one Samuel Shattuck, a Quaker recently banished from Boston.

⁓❦⁓

CHARLOTTE PERKINS GILMAN: THE WOMAN BEHIND THE WALLPAPER

The 1890s produced two rival images of the American woman. Illustrator Charles Dana Gibson gave America the Gibson Girl. Precursor to the Barbie doll, she was a paragon of femininity with her abundance of dark hair, her impossibly tiny waist and her Mona Lisa–like expression. Writer Charlotte Perkins Gilman's American woman wore a different expression: the twisted visage of the madwoman in the nursery. Independently, neither image likely embodied the reality of the twentieth-century American woman any more than a *Sports Illustrated* swimsuit model or an Amish woman would their twenty-first-century sister. Together, though, the Gibson Girl and the madwoman, and the polarity they represented, spoke to many women of the day, Providence's Gilman included.

Charlotte Perkins Gilman, writer, orator, publisher and feminist, was one of the leaders of the women's movement of the late nineteenth and early twentieth centuries. Her goal: a society that allowed women to be equal partners with men in domestic and professional spheres. As might be expected, she met with opposition from men and women alike. The aforementioned Charles Dana Gibson's Gibson Girl illustrations, for instance, held idealized beauty above all else, and occasionally his drawings bore anti-suffragette captions like "Not Worrying about Her Rights" and "No Time for Politics."

Gilman fought the vapidity of the Gibson Girl ideal for decades through her *Forerunner* magazine essays and manifestos like *Women and Economics*

Charlotte Perkins Gilman.

and *The Home*. Arguably, though, it was a single short story, "The Yellow Wallpaper," that made the most lasting impression on the public. This tale of a woman's descent into madness when her doctor/husband locks her in a room for enforced rest still rivets readers more than 110 years after its original publication. In "The Yellow Wallpaper," the main character is denied all intellectual stimulation and begins to believe that the yellow wallpaper in her nursery prison hides a woman watching her. Critics say it is likely an autobiographical story, having its germination in the days following the birth of Gilman's daughter, Katherine, in 1885. Horace

Scudder, editor of the *Atlantic*, said "that it was so terribly good that it ought never to be printed" and rejected the story. Fortunately, *New England Magazine* had lower standards, publishing the story in 1892.

A LIFE OF LONELINESS AND ISOLATION

Gilman, born in 1860, had a family tree that any number of writers would covet but a family life that few would envy. Through her father, Frederick Beecher Perkins of Hartford, Connecticut, Gilman was related to Harriet Beecher Stowe, author of *Uncle Tom's Cabin*, and Edward Everett Hale, author of *The Man Without a Country*. Her mother, Mary Westcott of Providence, was a direct descendant of one of the founders of Providence Plantations. A prestigious lineage does not a happy life make, however.

Gilman was the product of an absent father and a mother who withheld affection for fear that her daughter would later be wounded in love. In her autobiography, *The Living of Charlotte Perkins Gilman*, the author recounts a particularly painful memory regarding her mother's parenting:

> *Her method was to deny the child all expressions of affection as far as possible, so that she should not be used to it or long for it. "I used to put away your little hand from my cheek when you were a nursing baby," she told me in later years; "I did not want you to suffer as I had suffered." She would not let me caress her, and would not caress me unless I was asleep.*

A young Gilman's yearning for her mother's touch led her to subterfuge:

> *[I] did my best to keep awake till she came to bed, even using pins to prevent dropping off, and sometimes succeeding. Then how carefully I pretended to be sound asleep, and how rapturously I enjoyed being gathered into her arms, held close and kissed.*

In later childhood and adulthood, Gilman adopted her mother's philosophy about love and worked at eliminating all sentimentalism from her nature. She achieved a very lonely existence until meeting her future husband, Providence artist Walter Stetson. They had in common their artistic backgrounds; Gilman had attended Rhode Island School of Design for a time. The pair married in May 1884 and had Katherine in March

Wild Women

1885. Gilman suffered from depression during her pregnancy, and the birth of her daughter did nothing to alleviate it. By August 1885, Gilman's mother was taking care of the infant. Gilman tried various cures: a trip to California and a prescription of complete engagement in domesticity, no reading or writing permitted, by famed women's doctor S. Weir Mitchell.

Gilman's depression deepened, and she feared for her sanity. In 1887, Gilman amicably separated from her husband. Later still, Gilman would divide her family further. She entrusted the care and raising of her daughter to her best friend, the woman who had married Gilman's ex-husband. The public would decry her decision, but perhaps Gilman's choice reflected recognition of her own shortcomings as a mother and a desire to do right by her daughter.

Gilman achieved critical acclaim and public admiration. These reached their zenith with the publication of *Women and Economics* in 1898. Additionally, Gilman helped found the Women's Peace Party and saw women achieve the right to vote in 1920 with the passage of the Nineteenth Amendment to the United States Constitution. In her private life, though, it appears that Gilman suffered still. In 1935, at the age of seventy-five, Gilman, battling cancer, took her own life.

In death, Gilman would become one of the most celebrated female writers in American history. Author Joyce Carol Oates, in a preface to "The Yellow Wallpaper," notes that *Women and Economics* was regarded as the "'Bible' of the women's movement." And Oates says of "The Yellow Wallpaper" that, "had Gilman written nothing else, she would yet be, so far as a general readership is concern, as famous as she is now."

Within the pages of "The Yellow Wallpaper," Gilman's madwoman would challenge a patriarchal society that admitted no deviation from its strict conception of womanhood. Moreover, Gilman's madwoman illustrated the mental illness known as postpartum depression long before the medical community would coin the term. The Gibson Girl's power pales in comparison. Certainly, "The Yellow Wallpaper" must have brought no small measure of comfort to female readers who recognized themselves in the story.

As it does today.

JULIA WARD HOWE:
MOTHER OF MOTHER'S DAY

How much easier life would have been for Julia Ward Howe if she just hadn't cared. If she hadn't cared to write, her husband would have been so much happier. If she hadn't cared about matters of intellect, she would have been more readily accepted into Boston society. If she hadn't cared about freeing African Americans from the yoke of slavery, if she hadn't cared about emancipating American women from a system that allowed them no political power, if she could just have kept quiet in the face of war, death and injustice, how much easier her life would have been.

And how much poorer the world.

Julia Ward Howe, most well known for penning the lyrics to "The Battle Hymn of the Republic," accomplished a great deal in her ninety-one years. Howe was a mother of seven, a poet, an essayist, a lecturer, an abolitionist, a suffragette and the inventor of Mother's Day. In life, she associated with America's greatest intellects: Henry Wadsworth Longfellow, William Lloyd Garrison, Ralph Waldo Emerson and Oscar Wilde. In death, Howe keeps company with Bruce Springsteen, Carol King, James Brown and Bob Dylan as a member of the Songwriters Hall of Fame.

Her biography, penned by her daughters, won the Pulitzer Prize. Her example earned her the title "Queen of America."

Julia Ward Howe was born to poetess Julia Rush Cutler and wealthy banker Samuel Ward on May 27, 1819. Her father was a descendant of Rhode Island's founder, Roger Williams, and two of its early governors. The world of Howe's youth was peopled with the rich and powerful. Her sister-in-law, Emily Astor, was the granddaughter of one of the country's wealthiest businessmen, John Jacob Astor. Educated in private schools, Howe could speak seven languages. Howe's formal education ended when she was sixteen, but her interest in the study of language, writing and philosophy would last a lifetime.

In 1843, Howe married Samuel Gridley "Chev" Howe, a doctor eighteen years her elder, who ran the New England Institute for the Blind, later called the Perkins Institute. She had misgivings about the marriage, and they turned out to be well founded. Her authoritarian husband mismanaged Howe's inheritance and disapproved of her intellectual pursuits. The two temporarily separated in 1852 but reconciled when Samuel threatened to fight Howe for custody of two of their children. They had six children at the time.

Julia Ward Howe is buried at the Mount Auburn Cemetery in Cambridge, Massachusetts.

Howe wrote that her decision to stay with her husband was "the greatest sacrifice I can ever be called upon to make." A concession Howe was unwilling to make was giving up writing. In 1854, her collection of poems, *Passion Flowers*, drew critical acclaim from some and indignant criticism from others. Writer Joan Goodwin, in a biographical sketch of Julia Ward Howe for the Unitarian Universalist Historical Society, quoted a letter from Julia to her sister about her husband's reaction: "Chev was very angry about the book, and I really thought at one time that he would have driven me to insanity, so horribly did he behave."

Howe's husband would grow more temperate over time, Goodwin notes, but it doesn't appear that the woman ever won her husband's approval. A diary entry of Howe's attests as much:

> *I have been married twenty years today. In the course of that time I have never known my husband to approve of any act of mine, which I myself valued. Books—poems—essays—everything has been contemptible in his eyes because* [it was] *not his way of doing things…I am much grieved and disconcerted.*

Chev's contempt may have been difficult to bear, but its weight was not enough to stop Howe. There was another book of poetry and a play. She also wrote nonfiction, chronicling a trip to Cuba in the *New York Tribune*. Howe's greatest literary achievement came in 1862 with the publication of "The Battle Hymn of the Republic" in the *Atlantic*. Sources are not in agreement as to what the magazine paid for the priceless anthem of the abolitionist movement. Some say four dollars; some say five. It was this song that prompted Howe's nomination and induction into the Songwriters Hall of Fame in 1970, 108 years after its publication. The organization's mission is "to celebrate and honor the contributions of our great popular music songwriters who have written the soundtrack for our nation's history."

Howe's subsequent contributions to the formation of a national identity included her work for women's rights. She was at the forefront of the women's suffrage movement, co-founding the New England Woman's Club in 1868 and the American Woman Suffrage Association a year later. Howe also co-founded a suffrage newspaper. In 1870, Howe wrote her "Mother's Day Proclamation," a plea to the women of the world to advocate for peace, not war. In it, she exhorted women to rise up and

> *say firmly, we will not have great questions decided by irrelevant agencies. Our husbands shall not come to us reeking with carnage for caresses and applause. Our sons shall not be taken from us to unlearn all that we have been able to teach them of charity, mercy and patience. We women of one country will be too tender of those of another country to allow our sons to be trained to injure theirs.*

Howe held peace conferences in the United States and Britain and advocated that June 2 be designated an annual "Mother's Day for Peace," said her biographer, Valerie Ziegler, in her book *Diva Julia: The Public Romance and Private Agony of Julia Ward Howe*. In 1914, President Woodrow Wilson recognized it as a national holiday. Unfortunately, Mother's Day was four years too late for Howe, who died at Oak Glen, her South Portsmouth summer residence, on October 17, 1910. She was ninety-one years old.

In the last years of her life, Howe enjoyed the rarified existence that comes of being a national treasure. In 1908, Howe was the first woman elected to the American Academy of Arts and Letters. She was sought after by many for her opinions on matters of women's rights and world peace. In one interview, the former socialite was asked what advice she would give a young woman. Howe's answer, a scant ten words, aptly sums up her life's journey from pampered child of privilege to independent woman of substance: "Study Greek, my dear, it's better than a diamond necklace."

⊰❈⊱

ANNE HUTCHINSON: "AMERICAN JEZEBEL"

Though none ever charged her with witchcraft, Anne Hutchinson suffered as much as any of her Salem sisters and met an equally brutal end.

Hutchinson's admirers called her "saint," and her detractors, the servant of Satan. Massachusetts governor John Winthrop thought her an enemy of the state, a rebel who threatened to undermine the fledgling community that was Boston, Massachusetts, in 1635.

Hutchinson's crime: speaking her mind. Anne Hutchinson was a religious reformer, a woman who infuriated her Puritan community by preaching heretical ideas. She criticized the preachers of her day and advanced the preposterous idea that people could have a personal relationship with God. Hutchinson also held that God didn't like some people better than others, so the Puritans wouldn't be more favored by God than their Native American neighbors. Some say these ideas cost Hutchinson her life, which ended in the scalping and incineration of herself and six of her children at her New York farmhouse.

Famed American writer Nathaniel Hawthorne wrote in his 1830 essay "Mrs. Hutchinson" that she was a "woman of extraordinary talent and strong imagination, whom the latter quality, following the general direction taken by the enthusiasm of the times, prompted to stand forth as a reformer in religion." She was said to be the inspiration for Hester Prynne, the heroine of Hawthorne's most famous work, *The Scarlet Letter*. Like Prynne, Hutchinson was a strong, independent woman who incurred the fear and wrath of many for the crime of being herself.

Anne Marbury Hutchinson was born on July 17, 1591, in Alford, Lincolnshire, England. Her father, the Reverend Francis Marbury, a vicar and schoolmaster, taught his daughter how to read and write. Anne

Famed American author Nathaniel Hawthorne, whose statue is pictured above, is believed by some scholars to have fashioned his most famous heroine, Hester Prynne of *The Scarlet Letter*, after Anne Marbury Hutchinson.

had the good fortune of being born during the reign of the powerful monarch Queen Elizabeth I, whose example led many to educate their female children.

Hutchinson was twenty when her father, the Reverend Francis Marbury, died. A year later, in 1612, she married Will Hutchinson. They would have

Anne Marbury Hutchinson's memorial plaque reads. "Wife, mother, midwife, visionary, spiritual leader and original settler." *Photo by M.E. Reilly-McGreen.*

fifteen children during their marriage. In 1634, the Hutchinsons took their eleven children to live in Boston, Massachusetts. One year later, Hutchinson created the first weekly women's discussion group. It grew to be so popular that the group began to meet twice a week and extended membership to men. In attendance was Henry Vane, who became governor of Massachusetts.

The meetings, though, attracted critics as well. In 1637, Vane returned to England, in part because Hutchinson's adversaries found fault with his association with her. Hutchinson's chief enemy, then former governor John Winthrop, was reelected, and her fate was sealed. In November of that year, Hutchinson was charged with heresy, convicted and banned from Boston. Governor Winthrop proclaimed Anne "a woman not fit for our society."

The following year, Anne was excommunicated from the Puritan faith. She and thirty other families established the Portsmouth (Rhode Island) Compact, part of what would eventually become the state of Rhode Island and Providence Plantations. Hutchinson and her husband, Will, made their home in Portsmouth for a number of years until Will's death in 1642. Then Hutchinson left Rhode Island for Pelham Bay, New York, one biographer said, to put further distance between herself and her Puritan enemies.

Trouble dogged Hutchinson to the end, however. In 1643, she and six of her children were scalped and killed by Siwanoy Indians, who attacked Hutchinson's New York farm, burning it to the ground. One daughter, Susan, escaped death but was held captive by her mother's murderers for eight or nine years. Three other sons and two daughters survived their mother's death. Susan Hutchinson relocated to Jamestown, where she married and raised a family.

The first person to commemorate Hutchinson's life was the chief of the Siwanoy tribe, Wampage, who renamed himself Ann-Hoeck. Siwanoy tradition dictated that chiefs rename themselves after the vanquishing of their most formidable foe. Governor Winthrop sought to discredit Hutchinson after her death. Biographer Eve LaPlante writes in her book *American Jezebel* that it was Winthrop who first linked Jezebel, a biblical witch and whore, to Hutchinson. Such an epithet was the worst slander Winthrop could lob at Hutchinson. An idolater, the biblical Jezebel was thrown from her palace window and then trampled under the horses and chariot of an Israelite warrior. Like Jezebel's, Hutchinson's horrific fate was wrought by divine hands, Winthrop argued.

It would be over 250 years before Hutchinson would have her honor back. In 1911, New York recognized her as one of the most noted women of her time with a bronze plaque placed on Split Rock near her former farmstead. A nearby river bears her name, as does a major thoroughfare, the Hutchinson River Parkway. Massachusetts erected a bronze statue in her honor in front of its statehouse in 1923, and Rhode Island named a greenway Founders Brook/Anne M. Hutchinson Memorial Park.

In 1987, 350 years after her banishment from Beantown, Anne Hutchinson received a pardon from Massachusetts governor Michael Dukakis.

As for John Winthrop, first governor of Massachusetts, he inadvertently cast himself as the villain in Anne Hutchinson's story. In 1644, he published an account called "Short Story." LaPlante notes that historians who have read the account have described it as the savage work of a vindictive and malignant man. How pained would the God-fearing Winthrop be to know that this is his epitaph.

Ida Lewis:
Seafaring Savior

Anyone who has ever seen footage of a rescue at sea knows what a heroic feat it is to save someone from drowning. There might be any number of conditions to contend with, like riptides or great swells, stormy skies, frigid waters and, of course, panicky, drowning people.

Now imagine doing the rescuing in ankle-length woolen skirts and a corset. Such was Ida Lewis's rescue gear, along with a small rowboat, for most of her fifty-four-year career as keeper of the Lime Rock Lighthouse in Newport Harbor. In that time, Lewis would be called the most famous woman in America, drawing the notice of a United States president, society matrons, Civil War heroes and suffragettes. Her rescue efforts would be covered by the major newspapers of the day and noted by Congress itself.

Idawalley Zorada Lewis took over the work of running the Lime Rock Lighthouse in 1857, after her father, Hosea Lewis, suffered a stroke. She also took on the chore of rowing her siblings to and from their mainland

The Ida Lewis Yacht Club. *Photo by M.E. Reilly-McGreen.*

Entrance to the Ida Lewis Yacht Club. *Photo by M.E. Reilly-McGreen.*

school. The events of her life show her to have been a quick study; indeed, she taught herself to row. Lewis's competence allowed her father to keep his job until his death in 1872. Lewis's mother then received the commission. According to an October 22, 1911 *New York Times* article, Lewis was officially appointed lighthouse keeper in 1879 by an act of Congress.

A sketch of Lewis on the July 31, 1869 cover of the magazine *Harper's Weekly: A Journal of Civilization* was accompanied by the caption: "Miss Ida Lewis, The Heroine of Newport." The cover story, "Ida Lewis, The Newport Heroine," was published on the heels of her most celebrated rescue. During a gale on March 29, 1869, two soldiers destined for Fort Adams were clinging to their sinking vessel when Lewis's mother saw them from the lighthouse. When Lewis learned of their plight, she "rushed out without covering either on her head or feet, save a pair of stockings, and jumped into the boat," the *Harper's* article read. Lewis, who was suffering from a severe cold at the time, rescued the two. Moved by her bravery, the two soldiers later presented her with a gold watch. The nation rewarded her with unbridled admiration.

Ida Lewis never sought attention, but it doggedly pursued her. The national press couldn't say enough. Of one rescue during the winter of 1866, a reporter wrote, "It was a most daring feat, and required courage and perseverance such as few of the male sex even are possessed of." A 1911 *New York Times* article, published less than two weeks before her death, puts Lewis's total rescues at eighteen. The last was made when Lewis was sixty-five years old.

A 1911 article in the *Boston Globe* noted that Lewis "[held the] American cross of honor awarded in 1907 for the bravest woman in America." Lewis won many other awards, citations and medals, but the diminutive and demure heroine did not display these to the hoards who visited the lighthouse. In one summer, Lewis's father counted nine thousand visitors. Among those to pay their respects were Elizabeth Cady Stanton, Susan B. Anthony and Mrs. William Astor. Lewis even received a wedding proposal from President Ulysses S. Grant's vice president, Schuyler Colfax. She turned him down, saying she was already engaged. Lewis did marry a Captain William H. Wilson of Connecticut in 1870, but the couple separated within two years of the marriage.

Lewis's happiness was her work. In 1907, she wrote:

> *I am happy. There's a peace on this rock that you don't get on shore. There are hundreds of boats going in and out of this harbor in summer, and it's part of my happiness to know that they are depending on me to guide them safely.*

Lewis died on October 24, 1911, after suffering a stroke. The public impulse to honor the little lighthouse keeper continued after her death. In 1924, Lime Rock Lighthouse was renamed Ida Lewis Light. In 1987, Lewis was inducted into the National Maritime Hall of Fame, and in 2005, she was inducted into the Rhode Island Heritage Hall of Fame. The structure that was Ida's home is now the Ida Lewis Yacht Club.

⊰⊱

KATE CHASE SPRAGUE:
BEAUTY AND THE BEAST

Extreme cruelty, gross misbehavior, imprisonment, neglect, refusal of spousal support, consorting with prostitutes, sexually harassing the help and "often intoxicated, menacing, wild, and otherwise offensive" behavior—such were the claims Katherine (Kate) Chase Sprague lodged against her husband, Rhode Island's United States senator, William Sprague, in her 1881 divorce petition.

Sprague countered in his 1881 divorce petition that Kate had "kept company of, and been on terms of close and improper intimacy with other men," thrown her eldest child out of the family home, squandered the family fortune and repeatedly slandered him.

Such was the epitaph of one of the early Washington power-couple marriages that one biographer once described as "unholy." Myriad newspaper accounts of the day allege that the two had a tempestuous, vitriolic and violent marriage that was headed for certain tragedy. Kate Chase Sprague, however, was no victim. She would risk her life to save herself and her children from an abusive marriage, though it cost her social prominence and financial security.

When Kate Chase, daughter of Secretary of the Treasury Salmon Chase, married William Sprague on November 12, 1863, she was considered the second most powerful woman in Washington, D.C., number one being First Lady Mary Todd Lincoln. Kate was admired by Washington society not only for her beauty and wit but also for her political astuteness. She was her father Salmon's private secretary, and the primary goal of her youth was to help her father realize his dream of becoming president of the United States. Salmon did become chief justice of the Supreme Court, though the presidency eluded him. Kate's charm and magnetism certainly played a role in her father's success, and he did consult her on important matters. And certainly Mrs. Lincoln recognized Kate's prodigious powers. Rumor was that Mrs. Lincoln had forbid her husband from conversing or dancing with Kate, according to Peg A. Lamphier in her book *Kate Chase & William Sprague: Politics and Gender in a Civil War Marriage.*

The *New York Times* would hail Kate's marriage to Senator William Sprague as "a particularly brilliant match." Thirty-year-old William Sprague

Kate Chase Sprague.

was Rhode Island's boy wonder, a governor at twenty-nine, a United States senator at thirty-two. The "Belle of Washington," as Kate was known, and Rhode Island's former boy governor were Washington's young "it" couple. President Abraham Lincoln himself attended their wedding. Kate and William were young, beautiful, accomplished, successful and, as William was an heir to the Cranston, Rhode Island–based A&W Sprague cotton mill and calico-printing business, fabulously wealthy.

By 1881, Kate and William were the laughingstock of Washington society. She was cast as a conniving Jezebel, "a duplicitous, lying, cheating, and generally untrustworthy person," according to one biographer. He was an inebriated cuckold, a man of dubious political and business talents of whom the *New York Times* wrote, "In Providence and Newport he does not have the reputation of being a scholar."

William Sprague was reputed to take out his disappointments—professional, political and otherwise—on Kate, both in verbal rebuke and physical battery. In one instance, Kate would allege, he put a loaded gun to her head. In another, he throttled her and tried to throw her out a second-story window while their daughters looked on. Despite this, many Victorian-era women would likely have stayed in such a marriage, enduring abuse, assault and, in the most severe cases, attempted murder. After all, this was a male-dominated society, and a woman, even one as smart and educated as Kate, would have had few prospects for legitimate employment. It turns out that this belle of Washington had a backbone of steel, for she did what few women would have done. She left.

SCANDAL BY THE SEA

There is never, of course, any one single event that precipitates a divorce. Certainly, the dissolution of the Chase-Sprague union was years in the making. It is fair to say, though, that the final salvo in this battle was fired on the Narragansett shore at Canonchet. The $1 million mansion of Kate's design, situated on four hundred acres, was the summer home of the pair. "The Narragansett Affair," as some biographers called it, began in July 1879, when Kate and the pair's four children retired to their beachfront estate to escape Washington. There, Kate entertained houseguests, including New York State senator Roscoe Conkling, with whom she was likely having an affair.

Things heated up when William returned home early from a business trip. Unbeknownst to all three parties, William, Kate and Roscoe spent a night under the same roof. William learned the next day, when drinking at his favorite local bar, that Roscoe Conkling was at that very moment enjoying Kate's hospitality in his house. The Washington scuttlebutt was that Kate and Roscoe were three years into an affair, and William was incensed.

An inebriated William returned to his home to find Roscoe lounging on his piazza and Kate readying herself for an afternoon carriage ride with him. William threatened to shoot Roscoe if he didn't leave immediately. Roscoe said he would leave if Kate felt she was in no danger. Kate assured him that she had no fears for her safety, and Roscoe departed, but not before William and Kate's daughter, Ethel, flew to Roscoe, wrapped her arms around him and begged him not to go. Whether Ethel feared for her safety or her mother's is not documented, but her actions would indicate one, the other or both to be the case. Nonetheless, the senator departed, and within five minutes, so did William. Evidently, he was unsatisfied that Roscoe had left still breathing. Shotgun in hand, William set off after his rival.

William's next move cost him his public. Given that he'd discovered Roscoe in his own home, William would likely have been seen as justified in his anger and his threatening behavior toward Roscoe within his walls. But to take it to the streets of Narragansett was another thing altogether. Onlookers said that an inebriated William called Roscoe out to the street. The other man complied and tried to talk with William privately. The latter would have none of it. William told Roscoe that he would accept no apology and that Roscoe had better arm himself in the future: "I don't intend to shoot an unarmed man; but I tell you now that if you ever cross my path again I will shoot you at sight," he said. Newspaper accounts cast William as a hotheaded, intoxicated buffoon. He must have been incensed at the characterization.

While her husband was playing Wild, Wild West in town, Kate was making a fast getaway. She packed up her children and left Canonchet. She granted an interview about the incident to the *Providence Journal* and followed up with a lengthy letter. The white gloves were most definitely off:

> *As you must have surmised, Gov. Sprague's dissolute life and dissipated habits long ago interrupted our marital relations, though I have striven hard through untold humiliation and pain to hide from the world, for my children's sakes, the true condition of a blighted, miserable domestic life.*

Kate told a tale of marital woe, financial hardship, neglect and indecency. She called William unmanly in his personal life and unreliable in his business dealings. Moreover, Kate cast Roscoe as a family friend mistakenly accused of adultery. Mrs. William Sprague had the chance to preserve the honor of one of the men involved, and she chose Roscoe Conkling. William's humiliation was complete.

RECONCILIATION OR REVENGE?

Close friends must have wondered what could have possibly motivated Kate to return to Canonchet, and William, a few days later. Within five days of the incident, Kate, accompanied by a lawyer, and William sat down to discuss their situation. William stated his intention to take the children. Kate's lawyer advised her to return with the children to Canonchet. She did so that very evening.

Perhaps Kate feared that William would make good on his threat to take the children. Perhaps she feared that she would not be able to support them on her own. Perhaps Roscoe had prompted her to return to staunch the scandal. Or perhaps there was still another motive: retribution. The Canonchet house was filled with treasure: artwork, jewels, silver, all things that could bring a pretty price and, perhaps, buy Kate her freedom. How must she have felt when William led her to her sitting room and locked her in there? Kate kept her cool. After all, she had a rabid public in her corner. Newspapers printed stories of her internment at Canonchet. William, in what must have been an attempt to manage the media, allowed Kate one interview with a *New York Sun* reporter shortly after her imprisonment.

William had made another monumental blunder.

What Kate said in that interview is nothing short of remarkable considering she had said to numerous friends that she feared that Sprague was capable of killing her. She told the reporter:

> *I bore with meekness the unmanly sneers and reproaches* [Sprague] *showered upon me, not responding save when my children's relations to me were touched upon. I have my story to tell, and when the truth of this terrible business is known I know that I shall be justified. God knows that I have no reason to fear the truth, though for 13 long years my life has been a constant burden and drag upon me. For years I have had this thing weighing upon me, and have striven with all my might to stand between my husband's wrong-doing and the public. I have done it for the sake of my children, not for any affection that existed between us, for there has been none for years.*

Such a statement must have cost her dearly. Fortunately, her days with William were at a close. In her last two weeks at Canonchet, Kate managed to move out of the home jewels and other items with the help of loyal servants. William, for his part, continued with his carousing and drinking. The pair had one final confrontation during which William grabbed his wife by the neck and tried to throw her out a window of their daughters' room. Kate made her escape from Canonchet the next day, leaving with her three daughters while William napped on the piazza. For reasons unknown, she did not leave with her son, Willie. Perhaps this explains why Willie would choose to live with his father after Kate and William divorced.

THE AFTERMATH

Kate was granted her divorce, along with custody of the couple's three daughters. William had hinted that he was not the father of the girls, which might explain why Kate was awarded custody. Kate took the girls to Europe; Willie, the couple's eldest child, elected to remain with William.

For both parties, the divorce was the beginning of dark times, financially and otherwise. Whatever jewels and other items Kate may have managed to secrete and remove from Canonchet did not yield enough cash to keep Kate in her accustomed style. The great tragedy of her latter years had to be the suicide of Willie, her eldest son, in October 1890. She returned with her daughters to the United States to spend the remaining years of her life at her family home, Edgewood, in Washington, D.C. An impoverished Kate died at fifty-nine years of age on July 31, 1899, in her home surrounded by her daughters.

William's company, A&W Sprague, went bankrupt. Canonchet was auctioned off to pay his debts, but William and Willie, armed with rifles, laid siege to the family home, preventing the new owner from taking up residence. William stayed in his Narragansett home until February 1909, when the mansion caught fire and burned to the ground. The eighty-four-year-old former boy governor died in Paris in 1915 of meningitis.

One last item of interest: Kate Chase Sprague, in both her own *New York Times* obituary and that of her husband's, is praised as a singular woman. The *Times* said of Kate that "there was a magnetism in her personality, and the friendships she made were of the most loyal character."

The *Times* also notes:

> *She was a diplomat of uncommon tact, and within a short time the homage of the most eminent men in the country was hers. She was ambitious, and she wielded her power and the influence of her high social station as no other woman in this country has ever wielded such forces.*

William's obituary noted several personal lows: his twice turning to the shotgun to resolve disputes in Narragansett, his company's bankruptcy, a failed run for reelection and the suicide of his son. Of Kate, William's obituary said she "was accounted the most brilliant woman in the society of her own country."

A pity William never realized that his greatest asset was his wife.

BEATRICE TURNER: IMPRISONED PAINTED LADY

In life, Beatrice Turner was so arresting that she could attract attention even when doing something so mundane as mowing the lawn. She made a striking figure with her limpid brown eyes, oval face, bow lips and abundant brunette waves arranged Gibson Girl fashion. She left a lasting impression on everyone she met—both in life and death.

Most of Miss Turner's admirers made the lady's acquaintance long after her death in 1948. That was when the executors of Beatrice's will opened the doors of her Newport Cliff Walk mansion and found three thousand paintings by her hand and many of her image. The woman had painted her likeness again and again, chronicling her adult life on canvas and paper, seeking, perhaps, to find meaning in a life of loneliness.

Beatrice Turner was the only child of Andrew and Adele Turner, a well-off Philadelphia couple. Andrew Turner was a cotton broker who did well enough to afford not only their Main Line residence but also a home on Newport's fashionable Cliff Walk. The Turners bought Swann Villa in 1907 and soon thereafter changed its name to Cliffside. Privately, they called it Arcadia, a name that would have great significance for the family.

Beatrice Turner. *Photo by Mark Kiely.*

The Cliffside Inn, former home of Beatrice Turner. *Photo by Mark Kiely.*

PAINT IT BLACK

Beatrice proved herself to be a talented young artist, and her parents enrolled her in the Pennsylvania Academy of Fine Arts when she was sixteen. Two years, later, however, they removed her from the school. She had begun figure studies, necessitating the study of nude models, and her parents found this unacceptable. What Beatrice's father really found unacceptable was the idea of his daughter reaching womanhood. He forbade her to have beaus, or boyfriends, and, legend says, once punished her for strolling the Cliff Walk with a man.

Dad's interest in his daughter was unsettling to her biographer, Sheldon Bart. Bart, in his book *Beatrice: The Untold Story of a Legendary Woman of Mystery*, quoted a poem that Andrew had written to his daughter:

> *When looking at thy form divine*
> *Perfect in each curve and line*
> *And gazing at thy silken hair*
> *And basking in thy orbits rare*

Wild Women

A misnomer 'twas in naming thee
Aught else but Venus.

It can only be hoped that the penning of this poem was the full extent to which Andrew expressed such feelings toward his daughter.

In the days before his death, Andrew wrote another poem remarkable for its prescience. Andrew's words prefigured his death:

I dreamed that I dwelt in a house of black
Located in the land of Arcadia
And absolutely nothing did it lack
For I was with my two sweethearts.
I awoke and found I was in a house of brown
Far from loving glances and melodious voices.
O when we are so far from those that we love
Don't such dreams last until we meet again?

Andrew Turner's wife and daughter saw a directive in this poem. The "house of brown" was clearly meant to be read as the Philadelphia house. Arcadia was Cliffside, they knew. In his verse, Andrew Turner envisioned Arcadia as painted black. And so, they painted it. Black.

From the sea, it must have looked like a hulking spider clinging to the edge of the Cliff Walk. Painting Cliffside's façade black was certainly the most dramatic display of the Turner family's idiosyncrasies, but it was certainly not the only one. In fact, what the Turner ladies would do in the immediate days following Andrew Turner's death would make the painting of Cliffside black a mere footnote in their bizarre story.

Andrew Turner had a peculiar, but not entirely uncommon, phobia about death. He believed that his brother had been inadvertently buried while still alive and feared the same fate would befall him. He instructed his wife to be absolutely certain that he was dead before he was embalmed and entombed for all eternity. Adele Turner waited several days before allowing her husband to be embalmed and then several days following that. In those days, the deceased was laid out in his home. Andrew Turner was not interred until fifteen days after his death that September 1913. One reason for the delay was that Beatrice wanted to paint a posthumous portrait of her father. The burial's delay drew the attention of the *Philadelphia Inquirer*, which, on October 4, thirteen days after Andrew's death, ran a front-page article with the headline:

Dreaded Burial Alive: Keep Body for Two Weeks
Andrew J. Turner Died Sep 21; Funeral Oct 6
Recurrence of Dream of Brother Reviving in Grave
Haunted Cotton Broker

The decidedly morbid act gave vent to nasty rumors. One had the Turner women so attached to Andrew that they could only bear to have him buried in the basement. Another story held that Andrew's body hadn't been buried at all but was kept in an upstairs bedroom at Cliffside. How the Turner women would have managed to spirit the dead man's body from Philadelphia to Newport was a matter of little consequence to the architects of the tale. Newport society did not care to parse truth from fiction. The Turner women's actions were akin to social suicide; they would be treated as virtual pariahs in the City by the Sea for the remainder of their lives.

A LIFE NOT CHOSEN

On July 10, 1950, two years after Beatrice's death, *Life* magazine ran a feature on the artist entitled "Lonely Spinster Paints 1,000 Portraits of Herself." Beatrice outlived her mother by eight years and so suffered longest the malicious rumors and outright lies told about her. Her mother's companionship, though, may not have been a balm for Beatrice's loneliness.

The Turner women lived quietly following Andrew's death. Their public appearances were restricted to outings to the theatre and lectures at places like the Newport Art Museum. Beatrice, at twenty-five, recorded life with her mother in her diaries, dubbed *Daily Doings*. In them, Beatrice showed herself to be obedient but at times resentful of the many limitations her parents placed on her. Biographer Bart noted that Adele had, on one occasion, sniped at Beatrice, saying she could not live alone in the modern world. He quoted Beatrice's written response to her mother's charge:

Ma-ma says I'm a nasty little dog and that not being strong enough to fight the world I fight her. A charming speech, which rather proves that the modern method of fending for oneself and refusing to be tied down by one's elders has it[s] strong points.

Beatrice Turner and her mother. *Photo by Mark Kiely.*

Beatrice believed that her life had been foisted upon her against her will. In another diary entry, she wrote, "All my life I have done just what my family wished of me" and "I am leading a life I did not chose."

Perhaps if Beatrice had achieved acceptance in one area of her life, namely in her art, her story may have ended differently. But the people of that world seemed set on excluding her from becoming one of Newport's high society ladies. It could be that she scared them a little. Why did she persist in wearing Victorian fashions, for instance, long after they'd fallen out of favor? One neighbor noted that she would cover the handles of her push lawn mower with paper before applying her white-gloved hands to them. Certainly anachronistic in appearance, she must've seemed almost ghostly, a specter trapped out of time. Neighborhood children were fond of spying on the spinster, saying that Beatrice's house was haunted and she herself was a witch.

It can only be hoped that Beatrice found happiness in her art. Beatrice wrote that she sought as her subjects "faces with nobility of thought and character and earnest endeavor written upon them. Faces set immutably in their cast of character to be revered, admired and loved." That Beatrice so often painted her own visage might be taken as a sign that these were characteristics she possessed herself. Surely such a person would have achieved in life, if not happiness, then a certain satisfaction with how she had turned out. Certainly those who collect Beatrice's self-portraits now believe her to be a person of "earnest endeavor" whose face reflects "nobility of thought."

WILD WOMAN?

With her anachronistic wardrobe and antiquated habits, her reclusive lifestyle and shy manner, how could Beatrice Turner possibly be a wild woman? Sheldon Bart argues that the answer is hidden in plain sight—in the self-portraits Beatrice painted. Collectively, these are not a testament to female vanity but the product of a woman devoted to developing herself as an artist as best she could. In this, Bart argues, Beatrice Turner is thoroughly modern. The clothes and the manners, perhaps even the ebony house, were a ruse that fooled even Beatrice's domineering parents. In obeying her parents in small matters, Beatrice was able to achieve the freedom to do her art.

Much speculation has been made over Mona Lisa's enigmatic smile and what secret prompted it. The same questions could be asked of Beatrice Turner. And, like Mona Lisa, Beatrice Turner isn't telling.

⋯⊟⊱⋯

Edith Wharton: Exposing the Elite

Edith Wharton may have been a Pulitzer Prize–winning author, but no one in Newport would have trusted her to write its tourism brochures.

The city, alternately called the Queen of Resorts and the Sailing Capital of the World, failed to charm Wharton, who spent several summers of her childhood there, as well as a portion of her adult life. In her 1934 autobiography, *A Backward Glance*, Wharton wrote, "I was never happy at Newport. The climate did not agree with me, and I did not care for wateringplace mundanities, and always longed for the real country."

The first woman writer to win the Pulitzer for her 1929 novel, *The Age of Innocence*, Wharton grew up in Newport in the 1860s and '70s as a member of the Gilded Age society, which summered in the City by the Sea. As a child, she lived in the residence known as Pencraig; later, she made her home at Land's End, the façade of which she once described as "incurably ugly."

It was this second Newport house that prompted Wharton, with Boston architect Ogden Codman Jr., to write 1897's *The Decoration of Houses*, her first major work. Wharton writes in *A Backward Glance*:

> *Thanks to my late cousin's testamentary discernment my husband and I had been able to buy a home of our own at Newport. It was an ugly wooden house with half an acre of rock and illimitable miles of Atlantic Ocean; for, as its name, "Land's End," denoted, it stood on the edge of Rhode Island's easternmost cliffs, and our windows looked straight across to the west coast of Ireland. I disliked the relaxing and depressing climate, and the vapid watering place amusements in which the days were wasted; but I loved Land's End, with its windows framing the endlessly changing moods of the misty Atlantic, and the nightlong sound of the surges against the cliffs.*

Wharton also owed a debt of gratitude to Newport society families like the Astors and the Vanderbilts, whose characters and lifestyles provided her with fodder for two of her most celebrated novels, 1905's *The House of Mirth* and 1920's *The Age of Innocence*. The "vapid watering place amusements" of Newport's socialites were of the see-and-be-seen variety:

The regular afternoon diversion at Newport was a drive. Every day all the elderly ladies, leaning back in victoria or barouche, or the newfangled vis a vis, a four-seated carriage with a rumble for the footman, drove down the whole length of Bellevue Avenue, where the most fashionable villas then stood, and around the newly laid out "Ocean Drive," which skirted for several miles the wild rocky region between Narragansett bay [sic] and the Atlantic. For this drive it was customary to dress as elegantly as for a race meeting at Auteuil or Ascot. A brocaded or satin-striped dress, powerfully whale-boned, a small flower trimmed bonnet tied with a large tulle bow under the chin, a dotted tulle veil and a fringed silk or velvet sunshade, sometimes with a jointed handle of elaborately carved ivory, composed what was thought a suitable toilet for this daily circuit between wilderness and waves. If these occupations seem to us insufficient to fill a day, it must be remembered that the onerous and endless business of "calling" took up every spare hour. I can hardly picture a lady of my mother's generation without her card case in her hand. Calling was then a formidable affair, since many ladies had weekly "days" from which there was no possible escape, and others cultivated an exasperating habit of being at home on the very afternoon when, according to every reasonable calculation, one might have expected them to be at Polo, or at Mrs. Belmont's archery party, or abroad on their own sempiternal cardleaving.

Were she still living, Wharton would no doubt be one of those who returns calls at odd times, hoping to get the answering machine.

Newport's excesses may have aggravated Wharton, but the effect was much like sand to an oyster: a pearl resulted.

❧❦

SARAH HELEN WHITMAN: POE'S PARAMOUR AND PROTECTOR

Providence's Sarah Helen Power Whitman favored diaphanous white gowns and scarves so sheer they floated behind her, trailing like tendrils of mist on the heels of a ghost. She wrote poetry, admired the transcendentalists and held séances on Saturday nights in her Benefit Street home. The medium

Sarah Helen Whitman's portrait hangs in the Providence Athenaeum. *Photo courtesy of the Providence Athenaeum.*

exchanged white garb for black on such occasions and likely complemented the ensemble with a charm: a tiny coffin worn on a choker, a memento mori. Death was destiny.

Whitman was the heroine of an Edgar Allan Poe tale come to life. Certainly he admired her, proposing, as he did, after spending just three days with Whitman. But the poetess resembled the women in Poe's tales in more than just appearance. Whitman was an elusive prize, won and

Sarah Helen Whitman's Benefit Street home. *Photo by M.E. Reilly-McGreen.*

then lost by the famed poet and writer. But though Whitman could not commit to Poe during his lifetime, arguably she was most faithful to the man after his death.

It has been said that the woman known best as the former fiancée of Edgar Allan Poe sacrificed her own writing career to thwart a postmortem campaign to destroy the man known as the master of the macabre. Poe, credited with creating the horror, detective and science fiction genres, achieved literary notoriety and critics' animosity in his day. Brown University professor of comparative literature Arnold Weinstein calls him "America's most influential nineteenth-century man of letters" and "the most maligned figure in the American canon."

How did it happen that a widow from Benefit Street should become embroiled in such a controversy as that concerning Poe's reputation and, by association, his legacy? It started simply enough with a valentine.

In 1848, Whitman was a forty-five-year-old widowed poet and literary critic living with her mother at 88 Benefit Street. She wrote a poem titled "The Raven," the title itself an homage to Poe's masterpiece of the same name. He responded first with a copy of his 1831 poem "To Helen" and then

A tiny plaque affixed to the side of the house is Sarah Helen Whitman's only memorial. *Photo by M.E. Reilly-McGreen.*

with a version in Whitman's honor, "To Helen (Poe, 1848)." The flirtation in print continued until September 21, 1848, when the poet appeared at Whitman's doorstep. A three-day courtship, which included a date in a cemetery, ensued and culminated in Poe proposing marriage to Whitman, who was six years his senior.

Whitman was unwilling. In his article "Friends and Enemies: Women in the Life of Edgar Allan Poe," Richard P. Benton writes that Whitman likely wanted to keep things at the level of mild flirtation. Poe's reputation, after all, did not recommend him as marriage material. There was the penning and printing of his love letters to various women, for instance. This, on its face, does not seem problematic but for the fact that Poe was a married man when he first engaged in the behavior. While married to his cousin, Virginia Clemm, Poe had flirted in print with other women, themselves married. He even accompanied one woman to Providence while still married to his ailing young wife, who died of consumption in 1847. No evidence exists that these relationships of Poe's were physical, but they created scandal in New York literary circles.

Sarah Helen Whitman's remains lie under this modest marker at Providence's North Burial Ground. *Photo by M.E. Reilly-McGreen.*

Sarah Helen Whitman, being connected to the New York literary scene, no doubt knew of Poe's perceived transgressions. Still, she agreed to wed the man if he could agree to one condition: he must stop drinking. It was a promise he could not keep. On December 23, the eve of their wedding, Whitman received a letter alleging that Poe had broken his promise to her. They argued. She called off the wedding. He called off the wedding. Then Whitman, in an action that seemed almost a tribute, put an ether-soaked handkerchief to her face and passed out. Whitman's mother threw the poet out. Poe's last communication to Whitman was a letter in which he wrote that he would never speak against her. She did not return the letter, though she did return the favor.

Poe died on October 7, 1849, in Baltimore. It was widely thought that he drank himself to death. There was a new fiancée to mourn his passing and more than a few critics at the ready to malign him. Among them was Rufus W. Griswold, an editor and one-time rival of Poe's for the affections of one of Poe's married lovers. Griswold excoriated Poe in print. He wasn't the only one. Newport's Henry James said he thought Poe a minor talent. Griswold, though, had the most damning things to say, and Whitman went on the attack.

Wild Women

Whitman's 1860 defense of Poe, entitled *Edgar Poe and His Critics*, addressed the many charges levied against Poe—that he was immoral, perverse and cold; that he was cruel in his criticism of other writers; and that he was a hack incapable of expressing genuine sentiment in his writing. Perhaps this last charge was the most cruel, though the charge that Poe had hastened his wife's death by breaking her heart would also have caused the poet great pain.

Whitman's defense took on each argument. To those who would question his sincerity, she said, "We believe, too, that in the artistic utterance of poetic emotion he was at all times passionately genuine." As to the matter of his wife, Whitman offered compelling evidence: mother-in-law Maria Clemm's enduring regard for her former son-in-law:

> *We might cite the testimony alike of friends and enemies to Poe's unvarying kindness towards his young wife and cousin, if other testimony were needed than that of the tender love still cherished for his memory by one whose life was made doubly desolate by his death—the sister of his father, and the mother of his Virginia.*

Whitman's admiration of the writer even extended beyond esteeming his intellect. She attributed the following quotation to an unnamed source, a source the reader suspects is herself:

> *Everything about him distinguished him as a man of mark; his countenance, person, and gait were alike characteristic. His features were regular, and decidedly handsome. His complexion was clear and dark; the colour of his fine eyes seemingly a dark grey, but on closer inspection they were seen to be of that neutral, violet tint which is so difficult to define. His forehead was, without exception, the finest, in proportion and expression, that we have ever seen.*

Spoken like a woman in love, if not with the man, then with his memory. In response to Whitman's book, Griswold called Whitman insane and remarked that he had documents that, if made public, would harm her. Nothing came of it.

It is oddly fitting that Whitman's relationship with Poe should end as it started—with words of admiration. If Edgar Allan Poe is thought better of in death than he was in life, he owes this, in large part, to Whitman, the little-known poetess from Benefit Street.

BIBLIOGRAPHY

Bacon, Edgar M. *Narragansett Bay: Its Historic and Romantic Associations*. New York: G.P. Putnam's Sons, 1904.

Bart, Sheldon. *Beatrice: The Untold Story of a Legendary Woman of Mystery*. Newport, RI: Newport Legends, LLC, 1998.

Bell, Michael E. *Food for the Dead: On the Trail of New England's Vampires*. New York: Carroll & Graf, 2002.

Benton, Richard P. "Friends and Enemies in the Life of Edgar Allan Poe." Edgar Allan Poe Society of Baltimore, 1987. Available online at www. eapoe.org.

Berkin, Carol R., and Mary Beth Norton. *Women of America: A History*. Boston: Houghton Mifflin, 1979.

Bickford, Christopher. *Crime, Punishment and the Washington County Jail: Hard Time in Kingston, Rhode Island*. Kingston, RI: Pettaquamscutt Historical Society, 2002.

Cahill, Robert E. *New England's Witches and Wizards*. Salem, MA: Old Saltbox Publishing & Distributing, n.d.

Crane, Elaine Forman. *Killed Strangely: The Death of Rebecca Cornell*. New York: Cornell University Press, 2002.

D'Agostino, Thomas. *Haunted Rhode Island*. Atglen, PA: Schiffer, 2006.

Demos, John Putnam. *Entertaining Satan: Witchcraft and the Culture of Early New England (Galaxy Books)*. New York: Oxford University Press, 1983.

Earle, Alice M. *In Old Narragansett*. New York: Charles Scribner's Sons, 1898.

Gilman, Charlotte Perkins. *The Living of Charlotte Perkins Gilman*. Madison: University of Wisconsin Press, 1990.

Godbeer, Richard. *The Devil's Dominion: Magic and Religion in Early New England*. New York: Cambridge University Press, 1994.

————. *Escaping Salem: The Other Witch Hunt of 1692*. New York: Oxford University Press, 2005.

Griswold, S.S. *1757 Historical Sketch of the Town of Hopkinton from 1757 to 1876, Comprising a Period of 119 Years*. Hope Valley, RI: L.W.A. Cole, 1877.

Hazard, Caroline. *Narragansett Ballads with Songs and Lyrics*. Boston: Houghton Mifflin & Co., 1894.

Hazard, Thomas R., and Rowland G. Hazard. *The Jonnycake Papers of Shepherd Tom: Together with Reminiscences of Narragansett Schools of Former Days (1915)*. Boston: Merrymount, 1915.

Hoadly, Charles J. "A Case of Witchcraft in Hartford." *Connecticut Magazine* (November 1899).

Lamphier, Peg A. *Kate Chase & William Sprague: Politics and Gender in a Civil War Marriage*. Lincoln: University of Nebraska, 2003.

Laplante, Eve. *American Jezebel: The Uncommon Life of Anne Hutchinson, the Woman Who Defied the Puritans*. New York: Harper One, 2005.

Livermore, S.J. *A History of Block Island from Its Discovery in 1514, to the Present Time, 1876*. Hartford, CT: The Case, Lockwood & Brainard Co., 1877.

Pettaquamscutt Chapter of the Daughters of the American Revolution. *Facts and Fancies Concerning North Kingstown, Rhode Island*. Pawtucket, RI: Globe Printing Company, 1989.

Pezza, Kelly S. *History, Mystery and Lore of Rhode Island*. Wyoming, RI: Finca, 2006.

Pierce, John T., Sr. *Historical Tracts of the Town of Portsmouth, Rhode Island*. Portsmouth, RI: Hamilton Printing Company, 1991.

Plimpton, Ruth Talbot. *Mary Dyer Biography of a Rebel Quaker*. Boston: Branden, 1994.

Rapaport, Diane. *The Naked Quaker: True Crimes and Controversies from the Courts of Colonial New England*. Minneapolis, MN: Commonwealth Editions, 2007.

Ritchie, Ethel C. *Block Island Lore and Legends*. Block Island, RI: Frances M. Nugent, 1955.

Shelton, William H. *The Jumel Mansion: Being a Full History of the House on Harlem Heights Built by Roger Morris before the Revolution (1916)*. Boston: Houghton Mifflin, n.d.

Taylor, John M. *The Witchcraft Delusion in Colonial Connecticut (1647–1697)*. Charleston, SC: BiblioBazaar, 2007.

Uruburu, Paula. *American Eve: Evelyn Nesbit Stanford White, the Birth of the "It" Girl and the Crime of the Century*. New York: Riverhead Hardcover, 2008.

Vanderbilt Balsan, Consuelo. *The Glitter and the Gold*. New York: Harper & Brothers, 1952.

Wharton, Edith. *A Backward Glance*. New York: D. Appleton-Century, 1934.

Ziegler, Valerie. *Diva Julia: The Public Romance and Private Agony of Julia Ward Howe*. Harrisburg, PA: Trinity Press International, 2003.

ABOUT THE AUTHOR

M.E. Reilly-McGreen is an award-winning journalist and high school English teacher.

Visit us at
www.historypress.net

www.ingramcontent.com/pod-product-compliance
Lightning Source LLC
Chambersburg PA
CBHW060813100426
42813CB00004B/1052